Sweaty Stories FROM THE CLEVELAND SCHVITZ

JOSHUA WOMACK

Foreword by Samantha Buckholtz

Published by The History Press
An imprint of Arcadia Publishing
Charleston, SC
www.historypress.com

First published 2025

Manufactured in the United States

ISBN 9781467159142

Library of Congress Control Number: 2025943126

CONTENTS

Foreword, by Samantha Buckholtz 5
Introduction 7

1. What Is a "Schvitz," and Is It a Jewish Thing? 13
2. A Brief History on Bathhouses 16
3. Leaders of the Schvitz 27
4. A Hot Room in a Horrible Neighborhood 41
5. Why Is the Schvitz Predominantly a White Thing? 46
6. Features of the Schvitz 51
7. Why Is the Food (Especially the Steak) So Good at the Schvitz? 62
8. I Heard the Schvitz Caught on Fire. Is That True? 68
9. Did Any Shady Stuff Go Down at the Schvitz? 76
10. Schvitzies 82
11. Star Treatment 87
12. Ladies' Day 92
13. Public Enemy No. 1 97
14. Destination Wedding 100
15. The Schvitz's Future: A SWOT Analysis 104

Contents

Conclusion 113
Epilogue, by Samantha Buckholtz 117
Acknowledgements 121
Bibliography 123
About the Author 127

FOREWORD

Children love secret places. "This is my secret hideout" and "Come with me to my secret fort." I was born with a blossoming fascination with the imaginative, fantastical and mysterious. As a young Italian-Jewish girl from Cleveland, for as long as I can remember, I've been curious, fascinated and at times extremely jealous of the elusive "Schvitz."

My magnetic connection to the Schvitz began in utero. I am what my mother ate. During my gestation in the Gay Gold era (you'll learn more about him later), occasionally women would be welcome to the Schvitz, but only to eat steak. They would set up a little table on the fire escape or in another room, so no wives caught glimpses of naked men. My dad brought my mother, pregnant and hungry, to the Schvitz to feed her one day back in 1989. My mother, the sweet carnivore she is, needed to feed her growing baby girl a monster bone-in ribeye cut on the famous bandsaw. She could and still can eat any man under the table.

Growing up with grandparents who spoke Yiddish, it was commonplace for me to hear words thrown around daily. At home, *schvitz* was used as often as "mama" or "dada," so I cannot remember a time when I didn't know that word. My grandfather Norman was a longtime Schvitzer and an avid photographer. Next to his kitchen table in a sunny breakfast nook were countless photos of old men with potbellies wrapped in towels.

I never received an explanation on what it was, but I knew it wasn't really a girl's thing—except for a few hours on a Wednesday afternoon. Any time I pestered my grandmother to go, she scowled. "Now why would you want to go there?" she would say disapprovingly. The older and more rebellious I got, the worse my now full-blown obsession got. I'd pester my father, "Why can't girls go? That's not fair!"

"You can't always get what you want," my dad hummed as he jetted off to scrub naked men in a hot room for extra cash.

Year after year I was plagued by FOMO as my dad, my brother, my boy cousins, my uncles and my grandpa attended wild Schvitz parties. This budding feminist was not taking it lightly. "But…Mom, don't you want to go, too?" A hard no for many years. My dad often brought home mauled-over rib bones from the Schvitz trash to give our 140-pound great Pyrenees as a treat. Once I was so desperate to try a "Schvitz steak" that I took a garlicky bite from one of these previously eaten beef ribs—an embarrassingly nauseating thought now.

I was literally chomping at the bit to experience the Schvitz, my curiosity running wild. It's the same wild curiosity that Josh showed in writing and researching this book.

Whenever Josh would uncover some fun little Schvitz article or picture, he'd text me. My ADHD, stream-of-consciousness brain doesn't slow down enough for this type of painstaking research, but I'm glad Josh's brain did. The Schvitz's history needed a champion, someone who went deep in the steam room and metaphorically turned over every scalding granite rock to find out why men and women of all ages love this place so much. Josh's words resonated with me, and hopefully, they'll resonate with you. This is a book I've always wanted to read.

But enough about him! I left off telling you about gnawing at the rib bone from the Schvitz trash. Would that be as close as I would ever get to this Oz-like place? If I did get to go, how would I react? Would it live up to the expectations I had built up? Keep reading to find out, and don't forget to hydrate.

—Samantha Buckholtz
CNM
Cleveland Heights, Ohio

INTRODUCTION

In December 2023, I posted in the Cleveland Mob Facebook group asking for information about the Schvitz. I told them I was a local author researching the establishment for an upcoming book. I got one response, a surly one at that: "You don't want to know the things you're asking for and nobody will tell you. Leave it the hell alone and go away." Sir, tell me how you really feel. That's the last time I'll ask the mob for anything.

But I knew some old-timers would feel that way. The Schvitz is an enigma wrapped in a question mark and has long held the "The first rule about fight club is you don't talk about fight club" spirit. A 2002 article from the *Cleveland Jewish News* described it as "the secret, sweaty Jewish-Freemason club."

Whenever lists come out on what to do when you're in Cleveland, the usual spots pop up: the Rock & Roll Hall of Fame, West Side Market, the Metroparks and so on. The Schvitz isn't usually on these lists, and part of it is by design. For decades it thrived under the radar. You had to know someone who knew someone to get in. I couldn't believe nobody had written a book about this mysterious utopia located on the outskirts of town.

So, why write a book about the Schvitz? Is there an appetite for it? I could list a million reasons why, but I'll boil it down to three: sweat, stories and Billy.

Let's start with sweat. In my first book, *I'm Not a Copywriter But: Lessons Learned from a Late Bloomer*, I talked about how a sauna acts as an oil change for the brain, a place to warm your mind and soul. The Schvitz acts in the same manner, though with a different, more intense type of heat.

This page: The Schvitz in November 2024—a nondescript, utilitarian building tucked away in the Kinsman area. *Courtesy of the author*.

A good sweat relaxes your body, quiets your mind and opens your eyes. In the book *With Light Steam*, author Bryon MacWilliams echoes the sentiment: "I could almost fall asleep in this steam. I could, except I feel too alert, too alive." He expands: "Great steam, like great art, has the power to bring on the quiet."

Personally, saunas and steam rooms have helped me turn many bad days into good days. As a writer, I'm in my head a lot, probably too much. Sweating it out is like shaking the Etch a Sketch—a much-needed reset for my attitude and outlook. Now and then my wife will politely say, "I think you need to go to the sauna."

Sweat is a beautiful thing; ask the Romans. In Justin Glaser's excellent book *Sweat: Uncovering Your Body's Hidden Superpower*, he tells the story of Roman gladiators doing combat in huge arenas, sweating under the melting Mediterranean sun.

As an unlikely souvenir, the sweat of gladiators was collected and sold as cosmetic products! The sweat was gathered by using a tool called a strigil, a curved metal scraper that scooped up sweat and dirt from the skin. The sweat was combined with oil and dust from the arena and then collected and bottled.

Gladiators' sweat was believed to have positive effects. Women used it as a moisturizer, believing that when it was rubbed into the skin, it would enhance their complexion. It was also thought to have aphrodisiac appeal, a popular ingredient in love potions. As far as I know, nobody has ever requested the sweat from someone who's steamed at the Schvitz. OK, maybe Matthew McConaughey.

Secondly, it's about the stories. The Schvitz leaves an indelible mark for anyone who visits. There have been a handful of entertaining firsthand accounts. Doug Trattner's 2011 story in *Cleveland SCENE*, "Sweat the Small Stuff: Craving Steaks and Nakedness? Time to Find the Schvitz," not only brought to light what an experience at the Schvitz is all about but also got Trattner banned from the premises—more on that later.

When I interviewed people about the Schvitz, their eyes lit up. Like my high school friend Eric Novello said, "Old Jewish guys in Cleveland might forget their kids' names, but they never forget their first time at the Schvitz."

Many Schvitz regulars still reside in Northeast Ohio, and it seems just as many have moved away. Those who have moved always seem to come back though, at least once a year, to enjoy the pleasures of the Schvitz. It is uniquely Cleveland.

Above: The Novello brothers grew up on the east side of Cleveland. *From left to right*: Noah, Josh and Eric. Eric, with whom I graduated high school, has a Schvitz quote worth remembering: "Old Jewish guys in Cleveland might forget their kids' names, but they never forget their first time at the Schvitz." *Courtesy of Eric Novello.*

Left: A common scene at the Schvitz: shirtless men wrapped in towels, giving cheers to steak, steam and male bonding. *Courtesy of Jason Morris.*

Lastly, it's about Billy. Billy Buckholtz has owned the Schvitz since 2017, but his Schvitz journey started as a boy in the 1950s, when he was taught the art of the "platza" at barely ten years old by his father. "I stood beside him on the top step of the steam room, both of us with oak leaf branches in hand. He wouldn't let me scrub above the knees until I was thirteen."

I'm not smart or patient enough to write a chronological history of the Schvitz, but I did want to tell its history the best I could in an accurate, informational and entertaining way. Think of this book as a Schvitzipedia if you will.

Of course, this is a book about the Schvitz, but more importantly, it's a book about people's relationship with the mysterious building on Luke Avenue.

In 2027, the Schvitz will turn one hundred years old, and unlike a lot of things, not much has changed. Ironically, that's why people love it—and keep coming back.

This book was written for those who love the Schvitz and those who are curious about its mysteries. After reading, I hope the curious readers take a leap of faith to experience it for themselves. What can you expect? In the words of Billy: "The blessing of a good sweat and bath, along with a hearty meal and the magic of true friendship, stories and laughter."

Chapter 1

WHAT IS A "SCHVITZ," AND IS IT A JEWISH THING?

If you grew up in Northeast Ohio, especially on the east side, here's something you probably already know: All the Jewish people in this area are related to or know each other. It's like Six Degrees of Kevin Bacon or, in a more kosher sense, Kevin Steinberg or Kevin Goldstein.

Keith Arian, a 1969 Cleveland Heights graduate and president of the board of directors for the Shaker Historical Society, who used to go to the Schvitz every Thursday night with his father, sums it up nicely: "If you're a Jew from Cleveland and you meet another Jew who lives in the area, chances are he's your cousin, or you went to high school or temple with him. Or all three."

From the stories I gathered, going to the Schvitz was a rite of passage. Fathers would take their sons, and those sons would pass the tradition down.

"I have very clear memories of going with my father to the Schvitz, from a very young age, probably six or seven, until my late teens," said Daniel Rosenblum, who grew up in Middleburg Heights and now resides in Maryland. Rosenblum served as the U.S. ambassador to Kazakhstan up until 2025. He continued:

> *My dad, Lou Rosenblum, was a regular patron for decades, starting in the early 1950s up until around 2012, when he and my mother moved to Boston. He grew up in Brooklyn, so the Schvitz probably reminded him of his growing up, a piece of New York Jewish culture.*

I have fond and vivid memories of the steam room, watching the old guys who would go to the very highest and hottest step. As a boy, the whole thing seemed so mysterious to me. A lot of older men were speaking Yiddish, so I didn't even understand a lot of what was being said around me. And the ritual of going back and forth between the hot room and the ice-cold pool was very intimidating! But I loved the steaks and pickles and soda and the whole experience!

During the Shabbat or Sabbat, there are thirty-nine acts forbidden on the day of rest. One of them is heating water in the home. But the act of sweating—or schvitzing—was allowed.

Schvitz is both a noun and a verb. As a noun, it's a place or destination. Example: "My friends and I went to the Schvitz." As a verb, it simply means "to sweat." Example: "I'm schvitzing like crazy with this humidity." In English, *schvitz* is often used to refer to a sauna or steam bath or, more generally, the act of sweating.

Though the practice is mostly rooted in Jewish and Russian culture, you don't need to be Jewish or Russian to get in. Some long-standing Schvitzers almost feel an honorary conversion. "I'm the most Jewish-oriented Christian there is," laughed Richard Johns of Solon, who has been going to the Schvitz for decades. I relate to Johns. In researching this book, I talked to many older Jewish men, getting an appreciation for their jovial attitudes and appreciation for a tradition they hold so dear.

A cartoon of a man sweating in the Schvitz as another man next to him is snoring from the relaxing heat. *Courtesy of Ralph Solonitz.*

In the beginning, the Schvitz survived on a steady diet of Jewish immigrants who made Cleveland their home. Soon, the Polish, Hungarians and Italians caught on. Eventually, the Russians joined too, as they slowly left communist Russia. Still, the group that is most associated and stereotyped with the Schvitz is Jews, even making its way to the mainstream movies.

In the 1980 film *The Blues Brothers*, there's a scene with Elwood Blues (Dan Aykroyd) and "Joliet" Jake Blues (John Belushi) sitting with their booking agent, Maury Sline (Steve Lawrence), in a steam room. Elwood and

A humorous exchange between Sydney and Seth. Some people get it, some people don't. *Courtesy of Twitter.*

Jake are pleading with Sline to book them a gig, and Sline's character is the stereotypical Jewish businessman, cockily chewing gum and giving business advice to the men on a mission from God. The scene has a great ending, and if you're one of the few people who hasn't seen this classic film, I won't spoil it here.

Most of the firsthand accounts of the Schvitz come from Jewish men, who, as we mentioned earlier, came with their fathers and grandfathers. So is the Schvitz a Jewish thing? It certainly started that way, but the Schvitz has been enjoyed by more nationalities and, thankfully, skin tones in more recent years.

"I'm trying to de-Jewify the place," said Billy Buckholtz. "I want everyone, not just Jews, to feel at home here."

So is the Schvitz a Jewish thing? You could say it's an Eastern European thing, with the nationalities that originally went, going back to 1927. Today, though, it's enjoyed by more ethnic groups and races than ever. The Schvitz has come a long way.

Chapter 2

A BRIEF HISTORY ON BATHHOUSES

Believe it or not, the original idea behind bathhouses wasn't steak, steam and cigars. It was centered on community and cleanliness.

According to an article from Olympiadaily.com, the bathhouse ritual stretches back to sixth-century BC in ancient Greece, where bathhouses were constructed inside gymnasiums. Athletes used them for hygiene and recovery, but soon everyone was going.

Israeli archaeologist and educator Estee Dvorjetski writes in *Leisure, Pleasure, and Healing: Spa Culture and Medicine in Ancient Eastern Mediterranean*, "The Romans deserve the credit for combining the spiritual, social, and therapeutic value of bathing and exalting it into an art. Baths were the focus of communal life offering a place for relaxation, social gathering, and worship."

It should also be noted that bathhouses were used as a place for childbirth, mostly in Finland and Russia. In Finland specifically, saunas gave expecting mothers a warm, clean, private environment, which was considered ideal for giving birth. In Russia, *banyas* (a traditional Russian steam bath) were used for many of the same reasons.

The Russian banya experience is deep in mystery and folklore, one tradition being the bride's sweat being wiped from her body with a raw fish, which is then cooked and given to her husband to eat. Another extreme and painful banya childbirth ritual occurred in the early nineteenth century, in the northwest region of Smolensk in western Russia. According to William Ryan's *The Bathhouse at Midnight: An Historical Survey of Magic and Divination in Russia*, the man or husband would lie on a bench above his pregnant wife, a thread tied around his penis. "The midwife would then jerk the thread to coincide with the woman's birth pangs," Ryan writes, "thus producing sympathetic cries from above."

When I told my wife, Lauren, who is a doula familiar with the experiences of midwives, about this penis-tying story, she quipped, "I think that's a tradition we should bring back."

Community, Conversation and Fellowship

As for the Schvitz and bathhouse culture, community is the straw that stirs the drink. Unlike steam rooms and saunas in gyms and hotels, where people usually go for solitude and silence, the Schvitz is where fellowship is welcomed and expected. The conversations are lively, and you leave your ego and social status at the door.

"A funny thing happens in saunas and steam rooms. Men's pores open up, and so do their mouths!" said Leah Santosuosso, author of *East Cleveland*, who visited the Schvitz for the first time in 2024.

One frequent Schvitz-goer, who preferred to remain anonymous, described it like this: "What makes the Schvitz great is it's one of the only places left in society that levels the playing field. There's no VIP system." A popular Finnish quote from the book *The Finnish Way: Finding Courage, Wellness, and Happiness Through the Power of Sisu* declares, "All men are created equal, but nowhere more than in a sauna."

It's true. Most men who visit the Schvitz wouldn't be mistaken for world-class athletes chiseled from marble. The flaws (and flab) are out there in the open. Doctors, lawyers, union workers, mechanics, firemen and all other types of professionals sit side by side, shooting the shit.

"The term 'third space' gets thrown around a lot, but that's pretty much what the Schvitz is," says Eric Sandy. Sandy, who grew up in Rocky River and now lives in Cuyahoga Falls, finds the experience not only enjoyable but important as he gets older. A few years from turning forty, Sandy represents a younger clientele who appreciates the old-school guy time.

"It's easy to laugh off this idea of male bonding," says Sandy.

> *We kind of just sit around and talk about, well, about a little of everything and about nothing. The classic joke is that when we get home our wives ask, "How's so-and-so? How're the kids?" And we never really know, do we? We never got around to that, perhaps because we communicate in other*

Though the Schvitz is known for larger groups of men getting together, occasionally some come alone. Usually, those who show up solo end up befriending others over the shared fellowship of steam and steak. *Courtesy of Jason Morris.*

ways, speaking truths between the lines, revealing parts of ourselves with ball-busting jokes and easy small talk. The fast pace of our day-to-day lives doesn't leave much room for that, though. It takes a place like the golf course or a poker table or the Schvitz to ground us for a moment in fellowship.

Tony Vento, who grew up in South Florida and moved to Cleveland in 1991, was introduced to the Schvitz in 2008 and sees it similarly to Sandy.

"It's deeply rooted in community and authenticity," says Vento. "It's gritty but friendly. So much of our identity is wrapped up in our careers or our latest success or triumph. The Schvitz is where you go to give your amygdala a rest."

Vento's sentiments struck a particular chord with me. Years ago, I read *The Broken American Male: And How to Fix Him* by Rabbi Shmuley Boteach. The book describes the twenty-first-century rat race most men and women feel of go, go, go. Boteach emphasizes the notion that we are human beings, not human doings. At the Schvitz, you slow down to speed up.

"At the Schvitz, you are not your roles, whether it be a white-collar worker, blue-collar worker or whatever. You stop 'doing' and just 'be.'" Vento offers this wisdom: "Just don't do something, sit there."

With Light Steam author Bryon MacWilliams agrees: "In the steam room our judgments are tempered by having our physical imperfections open to scrutiny, and the futility of defining ourselves by the trappings of our roles in society."

The male bonding Sandy and Vento describe extends to the fairer sex as well. Amy Moniot saw a mobile sauna come through her Ohio City neighborhood in 2022, and a few of her female sauna-dwelling neighbors told Moniot they planned on doing a little field trip to the Schvitz for Ladies' Day for even more sweating.

"What surprised me was how the women I went with opened up, even in what seems like a vulnerable environment, said Moniot. "I feel like we shared personal things we wouldn't usually share. You get to know people very quickly."

Moniot's observation is shared by some noteworthy company, specifically Mikko Hautla, the ambassador of Finland to the United States. In the 2024 *New York Times* article "'Whatever Happens in the Sauna Stays in the Sauna': Diplomacy, Conducted in the Nude," Hautla elaborates: "When you are half-naked or even sometimes completely naked, it allows for deeper discussion. You talk in a way that doesn't happen when sitting around a table with a tie on or at some formal thing."

Mark Cousineau, from Shaker Heights, agrees. "Camaraderie is a big part of the Schvitz. Last year was the first time I went with a big group of dads from my kids' school. We normally see each other at kids' basketball games or Cub Scouts, and we are the kind of friends that just talk about the weather and sports. But to walk around in a towel lowers your guard. I had great talks with guys—finally getting over the small talk of our kids and talking about real stuff."

The community aspect can't be underestimated. "It's more social, less tranquil," says Steph Rienzi, who first went in 2024. "It's not like you walk into a peaceful atmosphere with a koi pond," she laughs. "But you still leave feeling great!"

Bathhouses in Cleveland

The Schvitz's original name was the Mount Pleasant Russian-Turkish Bathhouse and opened on Friday, November 25, 1927. The original address was 11407 Kinsman Road, and it was advertised as "The Finest, Cleanest and Most Sanitary Bath House in Cleveland." The Mount Pleasant Russian-Turkish Bathhouse offered a dry steam room, a small swimming pool, a restaurant and hotel accommodations with thirty private rooms.

The Jewish Independent, Friday, November 25, 1927; Page: 7

OPENS NEW KINSMAN ROAD BATH HOUSE

The Mt. Pleasant Russian-Turkish bath house, located at 11407 Kinsman road, is ready for business, according to Charles Sharp, proprietor. The bath house is complete in every detail and is one of the finest in the city. A dry steam room, beautiful swimming pool, a restaurant and hotel accommodations with thirty private rooms are some of the features. Mr. Sharp has arranged for plenty of parking space for his patrons.

This page: The first ads for the Mount Pleasant-Russian Turkish Bathhouse, opened on the day after Thanksgiving, Friday, November 25, 1927. One of the interesting parts of the advertisements is the hotel mention of the Schvitz, which was thirty dormitory-style rooms. Not many people remember the hotel portion of the Schvitz, but it was believed to be a popular resting place for traveling salesmen driving between New York and Chicago. The dorms also housed men who may have had too much to drink and perhaps a mobster or two looking to hide out. *Courtesy of the Samuel H. Miller Digital Archive of the* Cleveland Jewish News.

This page: The Orange Avenue Bath House opened in 1904 and was the first bathhouse in Cleveland to be run by city authorities. For two cents, you could get soap and a towel, along with a bath or shower. *Courtesy of Cleveland Memory Project, Cleveland State University Library Special Collections, and Case Western Reserve University, Encyclopedia of Cleveland History.*

The Mount Pleasant Russian-Turkish Bathhouse wasn't the first of its kind in the area, though. Cleveland City Council passed legislation in 1901 to address public health issues associated with overcrowded, unsanitary living conditions in the city's burgeoning immigrant neighborhoods, one of them being Mount Pleasant. Three years later in 1904, the Orange Avenue Cleveland Public Bath House opened at 1609 Orange Avenue. It was a three-story public bathhouse offering soap and a towel, along with a bath or a shower, for two cents.

According to Gail Greenberg's article from ClevelandJewishHistory.net, the Orange Avenue Bath House was constructed in 1904 and saw more than 113,000 people during its first year. The three-story building contained private and open baths, shower rooms, a gymnasium and a laundry room.

Another bathhouse from this period was the Morison Avenue Bathhouse located at 10606 Morison Avenue in the Glenville neighborhood. It was opened in 1925 and was the first and only Jewish communal bath built by an Orthodox Jewish community in the United States.

From 1904 to 1954, Cleveland operated numerous free year-round public bathhouses, including the Broadway (1906 Broadway) and the Clark Avenue (1908 Clark Avenue) bathhouses, along with the St. Clair Public Avenue Bathhouse (6250 St. Clair). The last bathhouse built in Cleveland was the Lincoln Park Baths (1201 Starkweather Avenue).

The Broadway Bathhouse was built in 1906 and cost $20,000 to build, serving the largely Polish neighborhood near Broadway Avenue and East 77th Street. Four miles away, the Clark Avenue Bathhouse, built in 1908 for $32,000, served the German and Czech neighborhoods on the near west side.

Left: The Morison Avenue Russian Turkish Bathhouse in 1950. *Courtesy of Cleveland Memory Project, Cleveland State University Library Special Collections.*

Below: The Morison Avenue Russian Turkish Bathhouse in 2024. The building was bought by the Progressive Baptist Association in 1954 but has been abandoned for years. *Courtesy of the author.*

As for the St. Clair Public Avenue Bathhouse, it was designed by city architect Frederick H. Betz in 1920 for $320,000. It held a large gym and swimming pool, along with showers and a laundry room. Cleveland City Council dedicated the building to Ray Chapman, the former Cleveland Indians shortstop who died earlier in the year when he was hit in the head by a pitch.

The St. Clair Public Avenue Bathhouse also has the distinct honor of surviving one of Cleveland's deadliest explosions: the East Ohio Gas Explosion and Fire of 1944, which happened less than one thousand feet

Top: The Clark Avenue Bathhouse was built in 1908 for $32,000. At the time, it was in what was then largely a German and Czech neighborhood on Cleveland's west side. *Courtesy of Cleveland Memory Project, Cleveland State University Library Special Collections.*

Middle: The Clark Avenue Bathhouse today. *Courtesy of the author.*

Bottom: The former St. Clair Avenue Public Bathhouse also survived the East Ohio Gas Explosion of 1944, which happened less than one thousand feet from the bathhouse. In 1977, the facility was named after former Cleveland Police Chief Edward J. Kovacic, who also served as the superintendent of the bathhouse from 1933 to 1934 and served on the city council from 1940 to 1953. *Courtesy of RemarkableOhio.org.*

A man inspects leaking water heaters at the Broadway Bathhouse in 1940. The city erected this bathhouse at a cost of around $20,000 in 1906 in a predominantly Polish neighborhood near Broadway Avenue and East 77th Street. It was the last remaining public bathhouse in the city when it closed in 1954. *Courtesy of the Cleveland Memory Project, Cleveland State University Library Special Collections.*

from the bathhouse. The explosion killed over 130 people and destroyed seventy-nine homes.

Why so many bathhouses? Cleveland saw an immigration spike in the 1890s, and many new residents didn't have plumbing or running water. According to an 1899 survey, only one bathtub existed for every six hundred Cleveland homes. Those who did have access to bathtubs mostly used them for coal bins or storage because they didn't have money for extra coal needed to heat the bath water.

Why did bathhouses go away? Eventually, indoor plumbing and private bathrooms appeared in American homes, especially after World War II. The early supporters of bathhouses believed public bathhouses would help assimilate European immigrants to middle-class American values, citing personal cleanliness would inspire self-respect and moral character.

Bathhouses were for more than just bathing, though. Of course, people went there to wash up, but many bathhouses offered ancillary features such as makeshift libraries and clinics. Families met up with other families, and the bathhouses took on the role of community centers.

This page: An Ohio Historical Marker that sits outside the former St. Clair Avenue Public Bathhouse, now the Edward J. Kovacic Recreation Center. As the marker states, the Bath House Movement was part of the Progressive era (1890s–1920s) in Cleveland to help address public health issues associated with overcrowded, unsanitary living conditions in the city's rising immigrant neighborhoods. In 1918 alone, the city reported that 482,000 baths were taken in the municipal facilities. *Courtesy of the author.*

Today, in true Cleveland architectural fashion, many of the former bathhouses have been repurposed. The St. Clair Baths now act as the Kovacic Recreation Center, named after Eddie Kovacic, the first director of the Recreation Center and councilman for Cleveland's Ward 23. City council designated the Kovacic Center a landmark in 1994.

In Tremont, the Lincoln Park Baths are now high-priced condos going for nearly half a million dollars. Dr. John Grabowski, Krieger-Mueller associate professor in applied history at Case Western Reserve University and director of research at the Western Reserve Historical Society, talks about the transformation of the Lincoln Park Baths in an audio clip from the Cleveland Historical website.

> *My favorite building in Tremont is the Lincoln Park Baths. We had a bathhouse movement in Cleveland, and elsewhere in the United States, because so many old neighborhoods at the turn of the century were not built with indoor plumbing. So suddenly, you had these areas hugely crowded with immigrants, and there's a hygiene issue.*
>
> *Today, the Lincoln Park baths are a set of condominiums which market at a price that would make an old Tremonter flip around. I find it ironic that a structure that was built by the municipality to give some sort of social assist to a community that was primarily used by several generations of millworkers—filthy, dirty, stinky millworkers—is now a $300,000 plus opportunity for a new lifestyle. That's just an absolutely incredible thing! It's just unreal!*

The interesting thing about the bathhouses mentioned here is how, architecturally, many of them have survived the wear and tear of Cleveland winters. Driving around and taking pictures of these buildings, it was obvious that the "bones" of each building are solid. Not even the huff and puff of Northeast Ohio winds could blow these buildings down.

It should be noted that many of the bathhouses that thrived in the early to almost mid-1900s were city operated. The Mount Pleasant Russian-Turkish Bathhouse was and still is privately owned. With changes in bathing rituals, entertainment and technology, it's even more remarkable the Schvitz is still standing nearly one hundred years later, full steam ahead.

Chapter 3

LEADERS OF THE SCHVITZ

The men who owned the Schvitz are as fascinating as the building itself, each one with their peculiarities and quirks. From laidback and quiet to crotchety and diplomatic, there's no one way to run a steam room.

The Schvitz has had just six owners since 1927. History has proved these guys are in it for the long haul. Like anything, everyone has their preference of what era they think is best.

If you ask eight out of ten men seventy or over, they might say the Gay Gold era was their favorite. Or for a slightly younger crowd, say fifty to sixty-nine, they might tell you they enjoyed the no-frills, shoot-from-the-hip style of Mark and Greg Balogh. Some like the updates that Billy Buckholtz has made, which include more frequent Ladies' Days, along with coed days, as well as building updates such as a TV inside the dining room, a patio outside the steam room, a new bathroom and showers and a new ventilation system (a result of COVID).

For many Schvitz-goers, the era they grew up in usually tends to be their favorite. And there's a certain sense of pride they carry, too. Everyone who walks through the door is a "steakholder," if you will. Billy Buckholtz sent me this text message in May 2024, which sums up what I'm trying to convey: "I hope that in your travels you've uncovered one of the most basic and universally magnetic draws of the Schvitz. You see every individual who comes here, past-present-future, feels a very personal sense of ownership: MY locker, MY table, MY pickles, MY towel, MY Schvitz."

Billy is right. Everyone who comes through the Schvitz doors feels a sense of ownership and, in a way, a parental sense of protection. Today, Billy is presented with the challenge of keeping the Schvitz alive and making the experience nice, but not *too* nice.

"I think 90 percent of what Billy has done has been great," said Alan Mancuso, health inspector for the City of Cleveland. "The building is cleaner now," Mancuso laughs. "And the menu is more broad." One of Alan's favorite additions to the Schvitz has been the patio.

"What a great idea, especially for the winter. You can go out in a towel or naked if you want, and those big heavy Cleveland snowflakes hit your skin. When you get too cold, you can head back inside and warm up in the steam room."

The 10 percent that Alan doesn't care for? "I could do without the TV in the dining room. It also seems like the cellphone rule is more lax now." Mancuso, in his mid-fifties, is a Progressive who is pretty open-minded about a lot of things. Still, there is an old-school charm about him that, like many others, prefers the Schvitz to be a place where you disconnect and let it all hang out.

"I'm not a fan of the coed days, but I get why Billy is doing them. When I go to the Schvitz, I like to steam naked, and you can't do that with the opposite sex around. But it's not a big deal; I just won't go to those particular days."

Going slightly off-topic here, I have to mention Mancuso's passion outside of the Schvitz and restaurant health inspections. Mancuso is a former proud goat owner in Ohio City. Back in 2016, he even used his goats in an attempt to break one of Cleveland's biggest championship droughts.

When the Indians played the Cubs in the World Series, Mancuso brought two of his goats downtown in the hopes of continuing the Cubs "Curse of the Billy Goat." Legend has it that on October 6, 1945, William "Billy Goat" Sianis, owner of the Billy Goat Tavern, arrived at Wrigley Field for game four of the 1945 World Series with his pet goat. Sianis, who had two box seat tickets for him and his goat, Murphy, was either turned away at the gate or was allowed to enter but later asked to leave because his goat smelled, according to history.com. Regardless, an angry Sianis allegedly declared, "Them Cubs, they ain't gonna win no more."

Mancuso was encouraged by his friend at church to bring his goats CC and Stardust down to Progressive Field to help keep Chicago's goat curse alive.

In an article from Cleveland.com, Mancuso said he thought his wife would nix the idea, but she was in. Mancuso and a couple of friends loaded up CC and Stardust in a minivan (filled with hay of course) and brought them downtown, walking outside the stadium and happily taking pictures with fans.

We all know how that World Series turned out, unfortunately, but it goes to show you some of the unique individuals in Cleveland who live and die by the sweat. All right, enough about goats; back to the Schvitz.

Mancuso isn't alone in his reservations about the Schvitz evolving with the twenty-first century. A big appeal is that it's one of the few places that hasn't adjusted to the times, and more accurately, it's a place where time stops. When you walk in, you feel like the event is something Don Draper and the ad men of Madison Avenue would partake in. It is old-world charm in a world that, for many, moves way too fast. In a way, the tension between both schools of thought keeps the conversations lively, inside and outside the steam room.

The question of what Schvitz owner was the "best" is like the classic debate over who was the better singer in Van Halen: David Lee Roth or Sammy Hagar? They both rock. And so have the Schvitz owners, each in their signature way.

Charles Sharp

The first owner of the Schvitz was Russian-born Charles Sharp, but the story really begins with Fannie and Simon Talisman.

The Talismans immigrated to America in 1907, and Simon quickly found work as a real estate developer. According to land transfers, Fannie obtained the property in 1917 and transferred it to Simon in 1925, and then Simon and Fannie transferred it to Midland Bank in November 1927. Two years before the Schvitz opened in 1925, Talisman sold bonds that were likely to pay for multiple buildings—one of them being the future home of the Mount Pleasant Russian-Turkish Bathhouse, which first acted as a synagogue.

According to permit 1398-G on May 27, 1927, the synagogue's use was to be converted to a gymnasium as Sharp was gearing up to open the Mount Pleasant Russian Bathhouse in November of that year.

Talisman founded five small synagogues in the Mount Pleasant area, eventually merging into one. As part of the agreement, Sharp let Talisman use the Schvitz to continue to hold services for his congregation. Though memories are few going back nearly one hundred years ago, some of Sharp's family still have vivid memories of the Schvitz's early days.

Left: The first owners of, at that time, the Mount Pleasant Russian-Turkish Bathhouse, Charles and Rose Sharp. *Courtesy of Alan Altshuld.*

Right: Alan Altshuld, great-grandson of original Schvitz owner Charles Sharp. Alan remembers helping his grandmother hand out towels and small bars of soap to patrons. *Courtesy of Alan Altshuld.*

"My great-grandfather was Charles Sharp. He came from the garment industry, as a coat cutter. I remember going to the Schvitz as a child and helping my grandmother Leah Sharp Lader handing out towels and a small bar of soap to patrons," says Alan Altshuld, who grew up in Mayfield Heights and now lives in Los Angeles.

"If I remember correctly, she paid me a dollar for my work. That was a lot of money for this kid. I also remember being freaked out watching men being whacked with branches! My dad, Jerry Altshuld, ran the steakhouse portion of the Schvitz for a little while, too."

Sharp, in addition to running the Schvitz, was also active in the Cleveland Jewish community, as a member of the Forest City Hebrew Benevolent Society, the Cleveland Hebrew Vilner Society, the Orthodox Orphan Home and the Yeshiva.

According to multiple interviews, the Mount Pleasant Bathhouse was built to serve the factory workers in the Kinsman area, a respite to wash the soot and grime from a hard day's work.

In a passage from Bert Stratton's *Klezmer Guy: Real Music & Real Estate* blog, he describes talking with Billy at a Yiddishe Cup gig (Stratton's musical group) and getting the lowdown on the Schvitz's early customers. "In the Schvitz's heyday, it catered to immigrant factory workers who dropped by after work to get the creosote off their skin, knock down a few shots and get a pleytse. The men didn't want to wait in line with their eight kids for the only bathtub at their house," says Buckholtz.

Isadore Lader

Isadore "Izzy" Lader inherited the Schvitz when Charles Sharp passed in 1943. Before he started a career in steak and steam, Izzy was a tailor, like Sharp, in the Cleveland area, mostly known in the ladies' garment industry. For more than twenty-five years, he worked for the old Korrect Coat Co. He also worked for F.H. Fellenbaum Co.

"Izzy was mild-tempered and among the family had a reputation as something of a saint. He had no hobbies other than a small garden and taking care of the yard. Did no formal exercise and smoked only occasionally. He would have a shot of whiskey every night when he came home from work," recalled Charles Mintz, Lader's grandson. Izzy's great-nephew Marc Seigel also remembers him as a kind man who would give all the kids silver dollars. He says, "I have great memories of the Schvitz; as kids, we all thought it was great."

Isadore Lader

Isadore Lader, a tailor associated for many years with the ladies' garment industry here, died Wednesday at Mt. Sinai Hospital. He was 70.

For more than 25 years, he worked for the old Korrect Coat Co. Most recently he was a tailor for the F. H. Fellenbaum Co.

From 1945 to 1960, he owned the Mount Pleasant Russian & Turkish Baths at 11409 Kinsman Road S. E.

Survivors include his wife, Leah, two daughters, Mrs. Natalie Altshuld and Mrs. Ravelle Mintz; a son, Marvin; two sisters; one brother, and seven grandchildren. The family home is at 4193 Verona Road, South Euclid.

Services will be at 1 p.m.

Top: Isadore Lader's obituary from 1964 shows he ran the Mount Pleasant Russian-Turkish Bathhouse from 1945 to 1960. *Courtesy of the* Plain Dealer.

Bottom: Isadore "Izzy" and Leah Lader. *Courtesy of Alan Altshuld.*

Though more detailed descriptions and stories of Isadore Lader were hard to come by, Izzy certainly played an important role in keeping the Schvitz going after Sharp passed. Lader took over the Schvitz just as World War II was ending. As soldiers returned home, they started families and could count on a good steam and steak.

JACK "YONKEL" GOLD

"The Schvitz used to be owned by Jack 'Yonkel' Gold. He and his wife Chika 'Ida' were close friends of my grandparents. The Golds lived upstairs from us in a duplex off of Kinsman and Chagrin in Shaker Heights for a few years when my brother and I were little. The Silvers and Golds! I remember going to, think it might have been the Central Market, with Yonkel, where he picked up produce for the kitchen. Mr. Gold used to bring home steak bones from the kitchen for my dog, Junior," recalls Paul-Jason Silver of Willoughby.

Yonkel was an original employee of the Schvitz back in 1927, so he was familiar with how the place operated.

Silver remembers growing up in the Mount Pleasant area and the Golds being like second grandparents to him and his brother Eric. "They were always very nice," says Silver. "My mother and grandmother would help the Golds out on Wednesdays for Ladies' Days at the Schvitz. You know, helping to cook the steaks and bussing tables."

Like Lader before him, memories of Yonkel are few. But the Golds' name in association with the Schvitz would continue on.

GAY GOLD

"Who's tougher than me? I'm a straight man named Gay who owns a steam bath for men."

Gay may have been right. To own a place that combines half-naked men brimming with testosterone along with alcohol and red meat does require a certain chutzpah. Gay took over the Schvitz when his father, Jack "Yonkel" Gold, passed in 1985.

Gay grew up in the Kinsman area, and by the time he was ten or eleven, he was already familiar with the nondescript building on Luke Avenue. After

Left: Gay Gold, mingling with a fellow Schvitzer. *Courtesy of Billy Buckholtz.*

Right: Gay Gold, remembered as a kind man who could say a lot with just a look, according to his daughters. *Courtesy of Billy Buckholtz.*

school, he and some buddies would run over to the Schvitz and do odd jobs for some of the wiseguys who hung out there, picking up their pressed suits from the laundromat, shining shoes and doing whatever they asked. The gangsters would throw a few bucks their way.

Gay Gold was a World War II veteran, serving in the army and navigating the jungles of the Philippines. When he came home, he bounced around with odd jobs here and there, one of his stops being a butcher. Needless to say, he took great pride in the steaks he served once he began running the Schvitz.

"I remember being no more than five or six years old, bringing my Matchbox cars into the steam room. I was only allowed to sit on the bottom step. There was a notorious Cleveland hitman who used to play with me and my cars. I was young, so I had no idea what his profession was!" says Brant Desatnik, owner of Dean Supply in Cleveland and great-grandson of Yonkel and grandson of Gay.

"I remember my grandfather's toupee and false teeth," says Brant. "His toupee was perfect, really!"

Brant's mother (Gay's daughter, Darcy Desatnik) remembers her father, Gay, as a laidback guy who could say a lot just with a look. "My dad never yelled, but he could make you feel about this big [pinching her thumb and index finger together] with just a look."

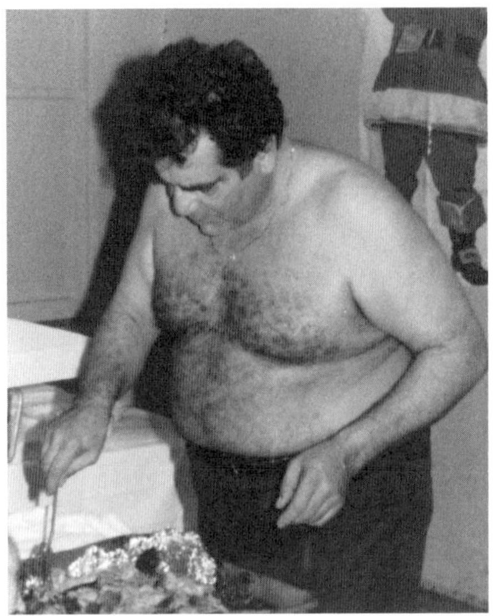

Left: Ernie Fisco, owner of Triple A Plumbing, enjoying what looks like a holiday dinner at the Schvitz with a Santa poster in the background. Fisco was a dear friend of Gay Gold's, and later, you'll see how he plays an even larger role in the Schvitz's history. *Courtesy of Billy Buckholtz.*

Right: Gay Gold's grandson Brant Desatnik and daughter, Darcy Desatnik, 2024. *Courtesy of the author.*

A Schvitz jacket from the Gay Gold era. "Hot Rocks, Good Times." *Courtesy of Jo Kirschenbaum Cowan.*

One story that both Gay's daughters laugh about is when Gay thought he saw a young boy smoking a cigar in the locker room. Smoking is allowed in the Schvitz, but Gay was caught off-guard when he saw a young man no more than four and a half feet tall walking by him, chomping on a cigar.

"My dad was laying on the cots, catching a quick nap, and when he opened his eyes, he saw this kid walk by smoking a cigar, knowing too well he wasn't old enough to smoke. My dad grabbed his arm, only to find Lil' John Rinaldi looking back at him!"

Though Gay preferred to keep the Schvitz lowkey and wasn't much of a promoter, there was one aspect of community involvement he was particularly proud of.

"The Schvitz sponsored a men's softball team for the Shaker softball league," recalls Danny Kirschenbaum, son of David "Doovy" Kirschenbaum, who we'll meet later. "I remember the hats; there were little herring fish on them," said Danny. "I know Gay really enjoyed sponsoring the team."

One of the endearing aspects of the Schvitz through the decades was its barebones approach to facility upkeep. The sheets and towels, exposed to intense sweat and thousands of washes, would eventually wither down, hanging on by a thread, literally.

Joel Kravitz, a regular in the '70s and '80s, remembers Gay's uncanny handyman skills. "Gay's idea of remodeling or improving the place was replacing a burned-out light bulb once a year. The place was perfect."

Mark and Greg Balogh

"That was the guy with the gun, right?" At least a dozen people responded this way when I brought up Mark Balogh.

Perhaps one of the most lasting images of the Schvitz, outside of the massive steaks and beer-bellied men, is Mark Balogh walking around the Schvitz, holstered at all times.

Graduating from Cleveland Heights High in 1971, Balogh was a former software salesman who also played bass in the locally known Mr. Stress Blues Band. But he was best known for running the Schvitz with his no-bullshit attitude. As was his brother Greg.

"Of the two, Greg was more vocal and Mark was more stoic," says Cody Cooper, former Cleveland comedian. "Neither were known for their

Greg Balogh. *Courtesy of Billy Buckholtz.*

diplomacy." Cooper, who has been to the Schvitz nearly fifty times since 2012, remembers a specific visit where Greg's personality was on full display.

"One time a guy was stumbling by me on his way to the bathroom that used to be near the fridge. He obviously couldn't handle his alcohol and ended up throwing up mostly on the floor, with a little of the spew landing on my leg."

Cooper remembers Greg laying into him, like a dad scolding his teenage son. "You dumb fuck, what the hell is wrong with you? How can you be this old and not be able to hold down your liquor?!"

Cooper recalls the man getting kicked out. Greg also knocked a few bucks off Cody's bill for the inconvenience. "It's such a unique place. I've tried to describe it to people, and the best way I know how is from someone on Yelp, who said it was a 'VFW Spa.'"

Andrew Zuccaro, originally from Highland Heights and now living in Columbus, remembers Mark Balogh well. "This one time there was a guy who was pretty drunk and asking Mark if he could leave his car there overnight. Mark told him no and that he didn't want people breaking into his lot to look through the guy's car. He told him to leave and take his car with him or call someone to bring a friend and drive his car home for the guy."

Apparently, the man thought he could convince Mark that the car would be fine. Big mistake.

"Mark kept saying, 'What do you think this is, Beachwood? This isn't fucking Beachwood. You can't just leave your car here all night. Get out of here.' The guy got smart with Mark and told him he was being a big dick or something, so Mark politely dragged the guy down the steps and tossed him out the door. The guy didn't leave his car there overnight."

But there was a softer side to Mark Balogh, who started coming to the Schvitz in the '80s and quickly developed a kinship with Gay Gold.

"Oh they definitely hit it off," recalls Darcy Desatnik, Gay's oldest daughter. "My dad said on more than one occasion that Mark was like a son to him." For Mark, the feeling was mutual in his fatherly-like respect and appreciation for Gay. Gay was getting older—he knew it and Mark knew it—so the elephant in the room was how the Schvitz would continue.

"There was some talk about my son Brant taking over, but he was only nineteen or twenty at the time and not that interested. After my dad died, Brant only went to the Schvitz one or two more times. He said it wasn't the same without Grandpa there."

Gay trusted Mark and knew he had the right demeanor and business sense to take over. Gay passed in 1994. A few years later, in 1996, his wife, Vivian, was nearing the end, but she knew there was one affair she had to get in order.

"My mom was on her deathbed, but she was adamant that I bring her the Schvitz paperwork, the deed or the title or whatever, to the hospital so she could sign it and make sure ownership was transferred to Mark. It was important to her that was taken care of."

Darcy remembers Mark as a kind and honest man who gave her father a lot of joy in the later years of his life.

"One time my dad was admitted to the hospital unexpectedly, and Mark was just about to jump on a flight out west. When he heard the news about my dad, he turned around, rescheduled his flight and came to make sure we were all ok."

Mark Balogh. *Courtesy of Billy Buckholtz.*

Another individual who saw the softer side of Mark was Kyle Wells of Lakewood. Wells's mother and Balogh dated for many years, and Kyle's formative years were shaped by the always fascinating Balogh.

"I never knew my dad, so Mark was the closest thing I had to a fatherly figure," says Wells. "Mark taught me a lot. On one trip, he showed me how to boogie board, and being a little kid that was really cool. We shared a love of Schwarzenegger movies too." A core memory for Kyle is being no more than six or seven years

RETURN ADDRESS:
SCHVITZ, INC
P.O. BOX 935
SHAKER HTS., OH 44120

OUT WITH THE OLD AND IN WITH THE NEW

Greg and Mark have changed the rocks in preparation for the 1996-97 Schvitz Season starting Thursday, September 19th.
As usual the best rib steaks, swordfish and chicken in the relaxing and casual atmosphere to which you are accustomed.

Regular Schvitz Hours:
Monday, Tuesday, Thursday & Friday: 1 P.M. TILL CLOSING

Wednesday and Saturday:
Available for private parties.

Return Address:
SCHVITZ, INC.
P.O. BOX 935
SHAKER HTS., OH 44120

CLASSIC ARCHITECTURE
FAMOUS STEAKS
SECRET LOCATION

The 1998-99 SCHVITZ season begins on September 22 at 1:00 p.m.

Regular hours: Monday, Tuesday, Thursday & Friday: 1 p.m. till closing.

RETURN ADDRESS:
SCHVITZ, INC
P.O. BOX 201822
SHAKER HTS., OH 44120

SEVENTY FIVE YEARS OLD? OUTSTANDING!

Come celebrate three quarters of a century of tradition in the original Cleveland location.
As always, Steam, Steak, Chicken, Fish and not so daily specials in our unique and relaxing atmosphere.

NEW SEASON STARTS OCT. 1st

The Schvitz is open Monday, Tuesday, Thursday and Friday 1PM to closing. Private parties available Wednesday and Saturdays by appointment only. Contact Greg or Mark for details.
See you at the Party!

Top: Postcard for the 1996 Schvitz season with Greg and Mark doing some maintenance in the oven for the steam room. *Courtesy of Billy Buckholtz.*

Middle: Postcard for the 1998–99 Schvitz season with the ivy covering the building. *Courtesy of Billy Buckholtz.*

Bottom: Postcard for the Schvitz's seventy-fifth anniversary, which would have been the 2002–03 season. *Courtesy of Billy Buckholtz.*

A Schvitz business card from the Mark and Greg Balogh era. No area code, no catchy slogan and, like the Balogh brothers, no nonsense. *Courtesy of Twitter.*

old, and Mark telling him to put on this heavy vest and lie on the floor in the backseat when leaving the Schvitz.

"I told my mother about that not too long ago, and she was like, 'I didn't need to know that!'"

Mark and Greg were serious about making sure the Schvitz legacy continued to thrive with the solid foundation Gay—and, before him, Yonkel—had built. In a fun piece of Schvitz history, Mark and Greg also hold the distinction of being the only non-Jewish owners in the Schvitz's nearly one hundred years.

Today, Mark and Greg's legacy lives on, and every now and then, their presence is still felt—and found.

"One time we were cleaning behind the kitchen oven and we found a case of shotgun shells," laughed Schvitz chef Paul Fierman. There's a good chance they belonged to Mark and Greg."

Billy Buckholtz

"My dad, Norm, brought me to the Schvitz when I was about seven. It was 1958, and the neighborhood was much different. Life was very different," says Buckholtz.

"The long deep case of sodas was a definite kid showstopper. My dad taught me to drink red and whites—that's cotton club cherry soda mixed with plain seltzer (two cents plain). When you finally drag your drained body out of the steam, your taste buds are super keen. Without the club soda, the cherry pop tasted like syrup."

Decades before Billy would take over the Schvitz, he was living the rock-and-roll lifestyle. From the mid-'70s to the mid-'80s, Billy was a member of the Cleveland rock group Wild Horses, where he played keyboards and sang.

Wild Horses was a workhorse outfit that played any and everywhere, from Spanky's in North Ridgeville to the Agora downtown. The band had a cult following, and in 1980, their most popular single, "Funky Poodle," was released and played all over Cleveland radio stations, as well as stations outside Northeast Ohio. As the music scene changed and bars began to change, close up or, in the Agora's sense, catch on fire in 1984, Buckholtz and his bandmates slowed down and eventually went their separate ways. Billy's got rock-and-roll stories, lots of them. But that's for another book.

For Billy's second act, he did what all rock stars do—he got into local politics. In 1994, Billy became president of Mayfield Village City Council. He had settled in Mayfield Village around 1987 with his wife, Michele, a Mayfield Heights graduate, and two kids, Mikey and Samantha. Michele has always had a political mind and has worked on numerous local campaigns. She encouraged Billy to run, knowing her husband had the unique combination of showmanship and street smarts.

One of Billy's unique strengths is his diplomatic nature, which undoubtedly served him well in Mayfield Village and has carried over in his final act at the Schvitz. Now and then, an ornery Schvitzer will scoff at the price tag of the Schvitz. Billy's response: "What do you want me to do?!" He asks the rhetorical question half in earnest and half jokingly. In the Schvitz, just about everyone gets along, but there are still egos and stubbornness. Billy is there to keep the peace.

"At the Schvitz, we don't talk about political, religious or social differences, unless it comes from a well-thought-out deep and historical standpoint," says Billy. And as far as the secret society reputation the Schvitz has had in having to know someone who knows someone to get in today, the system is much more relaxed.

Billy says, "When people ask me how to become a member of the Schvitz, I tell them it's easy. Just come here, walk up the steps, check in, have a good time and tip generously. When they ask how to become a regular, I tell them to repeat the same routine next week."

As you can tell, there's a connectedness to the Schvitz owners in terms of not only bloodlines but also tradition and respect. The five families of the Schvitz—the Sharps, the Laders, the Golds, the Baloghs and the Buckholtzes—have each played a part in keeping the Schvitz going, and each era has its own stories and warts. If you run into someone related to one of the Schvitz families, either at the Schvitz or somewhere else in Cleveland, buy 'em a drink; they've earned it.

Chapter 4

A HOT ROOM IN A HORRIBLE NEIGHBORHOOD

East 116th and Kinsman wasn't always a horrible neighborhood. Once upon a time, it was a melting pot, an eclectic mix of Poles, Italians, Slovenians and, of course, Jews. The Mount Pleasant area was once home to about 20 percent of Cleveland's Jewish population.

The first residents were Manx farmers who immigrated to the area in 1826 from the Isle of Man, an island located in the Irish Sea between Great Britain and Ireland. Mount Pleasant remained mostly rural until 1921, when Joseph Krizek and his partners bought twenty acres southwest of Kinsman, where they mapped out streets and planted 248 maple trees along Bartlett Street.

From roughly 1870 to 1914, Southern and Eastern European immigrants came to the area in search of a better life. Reasons included jobs, safety, religious freedom and family. The same migration was happening in other large American cities, too, like Chicago and Philadelphia.

One person who remembers the area of Mount Pleasant fondly is Tony "Doc" Sumodi, born in 1942. "It was a great neighborhood, an old-fashioned one. We were poor, but we didn't know we were poor."

What stood out to Sumodi was the diversity all along Kinsman Road. "Slovenians, Italians, Lithuanians, Blacks, Jews, some German in there, Croatian, Serbians—and surprisingly, they got along. The north side of Kinsman was predominantly Italian, Slovenian and Serbian. The south side was all Jewish. The neighborhood had these great stores—green grocers and open-air fruit markets, so during the summer you had all these aromas."

Billy and his son, Mikey, in the steam room. *Courtesy of Billy Buckholtz.*

In *Merging Traditions: Jewish Life in Cleveland*, the authors talk about Kinsman's heyday as being a smaller, more blue-collar city than its neighboring city, Glenville.

"Not only was Kinsman less developed at the start, but it was also smaller and had a greater mix of ethnic groups, mainly Italian and Czech, and most of them south of Kinsman. Also, a handy differentiation between the two areas of the second settlement would label Glenville as middle class and Kinsman as working class."

Sadly, Doc's and many others' memories are a shell of its bustling past. How did a once-thriving area deteriorate so fast? The short answer: redlining.

I felt embarrassed and naive, being in my forties and never hearing of redlining before, until a seasoned Schvitzer brought it up. There are much more researched and thoughtful articles you can look up, but here's a general description so we can apply it to the area around the Schvitz.

According to blackpast.com, "redlining" refers to a discriminatory pattern of disinvestment and obstructive lending practices that act as an impediment to homeownership or business owning among African Americans and other people of color. More concisely put, redlining kept money out of the hands of Blacks and other minorities, preventing them from owning homes or starting businesses.

The result is neighborhoods across the United States like Mount Pleasant. Banks would deem the areas too risky, resulting in vacant storefronts and blocks of abandoned homes. Blacks who lived and continue to live in redlined areas face the challenge of finding convenient ways to bank, get healthcare and shop for groceries.

Today, the area is roughly 95 percent Black, with fewer than fifteen thousand residents, and shows no signs of gentrification or substantial investment. The Schvitz's precarious location has led Billy to describe the Schvitz on the gut feeling he gets when explaining the place to newbies: "If there's someone I think would enjoy the Schvitz, I tell them it's just a few streets down from Shaker Square. If it's someone I think wouldn't be a good fit, I tell them it's in East Cleveland."

Everyone Stay Seated, Don't Move

Andrew Zuccaro remembers a night in the dead of winter when, for a moment, things got sketchy. He says:

> *A few years back, my friends and I were all at the Schvitz in the middle of a snowstorm. It was a cold December evening, and we all made a point to get there right after work because the roads were worsening by the minute. It snowed a full foot while we were inside that night.*

Anyway, we're all eating in the dining room when all of a sudden, the power cuts off and everyone goes silent. It was the darkest blackout I've ever experienced since there were no windows there. With your eyes wide open you honestly couldn't see the person sitting a few inches next to you. So, the lights go out, all is quiet, and then you hear a gun cock, and one of the previous owners, Mark, says, "Everyone stay seated; don't move."

He and his brother Greg found flashlights in the kitchen and slowly walked down the stairs to the front (and only) door of the Schvitz. You have to understand that the Schvitz is not in a good area of town and is a cash-only business. It isn't crazy to think they might be about to get robbed and someone cut the power. Mark and Greg also always had at least one pistol in each of their waistbands. They walked down the steps together, forced the steel door open through the foot of snow that had fallen and went outside to check everything out.

Luckily, they quickly saw that the entire block was out of power, and it wasn't just the Schvitz. They locked the door and came back up to tell everyone everything was OK, but we still had to sit there in the darkness for about thirty minutes until the power came back.

We'd always seen Mark's and Greg's guns in their waists and understood that we were in the hood, with lots of cash being passed, but it finally made a lot of sense and was all very real. Just another thing to add to the charm and experience of a night at the Schvitz!

Though part of the appeal of the Schvitz is its unique location, most would agree the area around Kinsman Road isn't one you want to hang around. It's understood that going to the Schvitz is a get-in-and-get-out type of commute.

Police Escort

"I had just finished up working at the Schvitz on I think a Friday night in the dead of winter," says Kevin "Noodles" Lynch, who at the time was one of the masseurs. "There was nobody on the road, and for some reason, I was booking it, doing about sixty on Kinsman where the speed limit is thirty-five. In my rearview mirror, I see the flashing blue lights and get pulled over.

"The cop walks up as I lower my window. 'Sir, you were driving pretty fast there if you didn't know.'" Lynch responded with "Sorry, officer, I just finished up work and am just trying to get out of this area to head home."

The officer, surprised that Lynch said he worked in the area, asked for some more information. "Really, you work over here? Where at?" to which Lynch responded with the Schvitz. Still skeptical about why Lynch, a young man of Thai descent, was driving through the neighborhood, he followed up his question with another question. "Oh, the Schvitz? How are the owners doing over there?"

At this point, Lynch knew the officer was testing him. The cop was probably waiting for Lynch to nervously give a vague response. Lynch picked up on what was happening.

"Oh, Mark and Greg? They're doing great." Luckily, those were the names the officer wanted to hear. After taking Lynch's license and registration back to the squad car, the officer shortly returned to Lynch and his car, handed back the license and registration, sans ticket, and told Lynch, "Follow me."

"Next thing I know is the officer throws on his lights and sirens and together we're flying down Kinsman. I was right behind him, and I couldn't believe it. My very own police escort!" laughed Lynch.

"He took me all the way down to the 490 on-ramp, and when I passed him, he gave me a sort of tip-of-the-cap salute. One of the coolest things I've experienced. When I got home, I called my brother and excitedly told him what happened. The next day I told Mark and Greg."

Mark and Greg asked what the officer looked like. When Lynch described him to the Balogh brothers, they were familiar with him. Chances are the officer had been in for a steak and a steam before. In a little piece of fun Schvitz history, there was actually a meal that was made specifically for law enforcement when they would stop by.

"Before Cleveland police cruisers had tracking systems on their cars, one of their favorite spots to stop for lunch was the Schvitz," says Billy Buckholtz. According to Billy, patrolmen and detectives would swing by for the "detective cut," which was a thinner slice of steak that could be cooked up quickly. Did the officers and detectives stay for a steam, too? Most didn't; that would be pushing it.

Chapter 5

WHY IS THE SCHVITZ PREDOMINANTLY A WHITE THING?

Malik Moore was running the YMCA in Cleveland on Prospect Avenue when a man approached him with a bloody face resulting from an intense game of racquetball. The man was Alan Mancuso, the goat farmer we met earlier.

After Moore helped clean up Mancuso with a first-aid kit, the two got to talking. They hit it off, and before they parted ways, Mancuso asked Moore, "You wanna get naked with me and eat meat?" Mancuso explained the Schvitz to Moore, describing it as a Cleveland treasure he had to experience.

"I had heard mentions of the Schvitz now and then," said Moore. Moore, who grew up in Philadelphia, came to Cleveland in 2007 and met Mancuso in 2010. "I had been to the Jewish Y in Philadelphia, so I was familiar with steam rooms in gym settings, but nothing could prepare me for the Schvitz."

Moore is African American. When he walked into the Schvitz with Mancuso, he immediately felt at home. "I was blown away. In the dining room alone, you could hear conversations taking place in three different languages."

Mancuso brought Mark and Greg to the side and explained how he knew Moore, vouching for his character and company. Was Moore the only Black guest at the Schvitz that day? Probably. That month? There's a good chance. As Malik sat down in the dining room, his towel wasn't fully covering his groin area. Mark always noticed when a stray wiener was flying or a bare bottom was on one of the dining room chairs. Mark playfully quipped to Malik, "Hey, we serve steaks here, not sausages!" This type of banter was and still is a rite of passage in Schvitz culture.

The relationship between the Schvitz and African Americans is a complicated one. If there's a proverbial elephant in the steam room, it's the lack of diversity the Schvitz has historically drawn. Charles Mintz, the great-grandson of original Schvitz owner Charles Sharp, recognizes the juxtaposition: "There was and still is a disconnect between the patrons and the neighborhood. Not a good sign."

One thing to keep in mind is that when the Schvitz opened in 1927, the area looked a lot different. Eastern European immigrants, many of them Jewish, Polish and Hungarian, made up the majority of the population in the Kinsman and Mount Pleasant area. After World War II, many residents moved east to places like University Heights, Cleveland Heights and Beachwood. When African Americans began planting roots, the Schvitz became one of those places in the area you just kind of left alone.

"There's a good chance if you're over sixty-five and Black and you've grown up near the Schvitz, you have your conceptions or misconceptions about it," says Moore. "There's a good chance those men, many of them now grandfathers, passed their own opinions down to their sons and grandsons. So naturally, those generations have stayed away, too."

One Schvitzer told me about a mantra or saying he overheard as it pertained to the old ways of the Schvitz. "No bros, No hos, No mos"—

Mikey Buckholtz and his grandfather Alan. *Courtesy of Billy Buckholtz.*

One of the few remnants of the fire, the sign that used to sit atop the Schvitz symbolizing the year it was started, in 1927. *Courtesy of Billy Buckholtz.*

meaning no Blacks, women or homosexuals. It's tough to say if this was a widespread notion, but bigots are everywhere, not just in bathhouses.

Moore is correct in his guess. The dynamic between the Schvitz and the community is twofold: Historically, the Schvitz never went out of its way to educate the community on what it's all about, and by the same token, the community never went out of its way to learn about the secretive building on Luke Avenue.

Though it's not a cut-and-dry, apples-to-apples comparison, one can look just three hours away to see a similar dilemma in another one of America's rustbelt cities.

The three-story, twelve-thousand-square-foot Detroit Schvitz opened around 1918. As the area around the Detroit Schvitz (originally called the Oakland Baths or the Oakland Bathhouse) changed, so did the misconceptions about what went on inside.

Paddy Lynch, a third-generation son of Lynch & Sons Funeral Directors, bought the Detroit Schvitz in 2017 for $160,000 when he was just thirty-three. Immediately, he knew the importance of educating the community on what the Schvitz was now and what it would look like moving forward.

"I was lucky; when I was little, my parents would take me to downtown Detroit, even to some seedy parts, so I didn't grow up afraid of certain areas," said Lynch. "With my family's funeral business, the majority of our clientele was white, but we handled some Black funerals, too. My dad was friends with a few of the Black funeral directors in the area as well."

When Lynch took over the Detroit Schvitz, one of his goals was community outreach. "We share a parking lot with Nazarene Missionary Church, a Baptist church just a few minutes away. It was important to me to let the congregation know this was an inclusive place, not just for Blacks but for women, trans-people and nonbinary as well."

Jessi Nigl, one of Lynch's business partners in the Schvitz, heard feedback from the community that sounds similar to the hypothesis Malik Moore proposed earlier. "Some of the people in the Oakland community we've reached out to were like, 'I can't believe I'm in this building. We thought we'd never go in this place; our grandmothers always told us to cross the street when you walk by there....That place is filled with dangerous white men,'" said Nigl.

The Detroit Schvitz opened around 1918 and was originally called the Oakland Baths or the Oakland Bathhouse. The building is twelve thousand square feet and three stories tall. Like the Cleveland Schvitz, the area around it has changed, but it has experienced a resurgence since Paddy Lynch bought the building for $160,000 in 2017. *Courtesy of Michelle Gerard and Jenna Belevender.*

Today, the Cleveland Schvitz is slowly expanding its reach. Luckily, Billy is a people person and a promoter.

"I met Billy my first year in office, and he gave me a great tour of the place," said Deborah Gray, councilwoman of Ward 4. "I can't wait to spend a full day there with my friends to enjoy everything he has done with it."

Not everyone has had the same pleasant experience as Gray. In a response to Jeffrey Levick's article "Sweatin' with the Oldies" in the *Cleveland Jewish News* in 2002, Arthur Lavin, a Caucasian retired pediatrician and applied neurosurgeon from Shaker Heights, said he experienced a little friction when he looked to bring a group to the Schvitz.

> *I only wish virtues of the Schvitz were true. A policy that nullifies whatever joy can be found there is that it excludes at least one ethnic group, African Americans.*
>
> *A few years ago, I called to reserve some time at the Cleveland Schvitz, and the call was going very well until I mentioned that some in our party were African Americans. Suddenly I was told that you had to be a member to visit. I then asked how one becomes a member and was told that there was a long waiting list. I was left with the impression that African Americans were specifically not welcome.*
>
> *I like the concept of a Schvitz, but nostalgia cannot blur the tragedy of racism, and even a nice trip down memory lane cannot justify our support of a profound and fundamental wrong.*

If you look at things from a glass-half-full perspective, it's encouraging that today the Schvitz is a welcoming, inclusive environment. It will still take some time to rid the reputation built up over nearly one hundred years, but it looks promising. In Alcoholics Anonymous, the slogan is "One day at a time." For the Schvitz and its future, it will be men and women of all skin tones experiencing the Schvitz for themselves, one steam at a time.

Chapter 6

FEATURES OF THE SCHVITZ

For Schvitz veterans, a description of the different types of heat might seem like child's play, but to appreciate the distinct steam the Schvitz produces, it's good to start with the basics.

Saunas, as most people know, offer a dry heat made of wood (popular wood choices include cedar, hemlock and aspen) and usually use a heat source to warm the air in the room, which in turn warms your body and makes you sweat. The wood absorbs the moisture, providing a dry environment.

In a sauna, temperatures can range from 140 to 200 degrees Fahrenheit (70 to 90 degrees Celsius), with a humidity level of 5 to 30 percent. Though the research is still in its infancy, the benefits of multiple sauna sessions per week include increased blood circulation and metabolism, weight loss (mostly water weight), muscle and joint pain relief and relaxation.

Steam rooms, on the other hand, are made of ceramic tile or plastic and use a generator to heat water into steam, releasing it into the air and making the environment very hot and humid. In a steam room, temperatures can range from about 110 to 120 degrees Fahrenheit (45 to 50 degrees Celsius), but the humidity can reach 100 percent. The same benefits are offered as a sauna, but steam rooms can also aid in upper respiratory symptoms by loosening mucus and phlegm. For those with sinus and allergy issues, the steam room might be the next best thing to a neti pot!

The heat, or steam, produced at the Schvitz is its own sweltering, intense animal. As Billy has said, "This steam is the *only* steam. Not as dry as a sauna, but not as wet as a steam room."

BY CHRISTOPHER EVANS

Where Guys Go

In a bricked-up brick building at the end of a dead-end road that cuts through a Cleveland neighborhood so old and withered it should have died a long, long time ago, is a place of shadows and steam and steaks, where men can be men, and the only women are bare-breasted and Scotch-taped to the walls.

This is the *schvitz*, a Yiddish word meaning steam bath, and it has been here off Kinsman since the 1920s, a private place, a secret place, well-hidden and guarded and pretty much unchanged except for the prices and the new indoor/outdoor carpeting in the plywood-paneled dining room.

The entrance is in the back, off a fenced-in, unpaved parking lot, and the first thing you notice when you step inside is the darkness. You are in a small hallway that opens up into a large room lined on both sides with waist-high cots where men sleep, open-mouthed and snoring, curled in towels and sheets. The only light spills from the dining room around the corner.

There is an unlit walk-in linen closet to your immediate left, and what you do is grab a couple of towels and a bedsheet. As you walk between the cots, the men in the dining room, big-bellied and burping, bath towels tucked neatly around their waists, turn to watch you.

In the gloom, two rubdown tables have been set up. On one of them, Alan has his thumbs buried deep in some guy's back, the bones crunching like dry cereal. His rubdowns last about half an hour. He goes from the top of your head to the tip of your toes (and that includes your nose) for $8.

A single light bulb illuminates the lockers. They are painted green and look like they have been drop-kicked from a great height. Here you undress, and even though the lockers have locks, few use them. Nobody steals in a *schvitz*. It is unthinkable. Like ferns, or instruments of exercise, or Muzak, or track lighting, or anything else you might expect in a steam bath.

Once you're naked, you're ready. You step through a door off the bathroom into the bright lights of a shower room so cavernous you expect to see stalactites. It's very spartan, no stalls, just a row of shower heads along the wall. They end near another door and — leaving your towel outside — you step into the *schvitz*.

It is high-ceilinged and huge, well-lit; the tile floor is slippery. On your right, five rows of what look like wooden bleachers rise and run the entire length of the room. On your left are the ovens. They take up the whole wall, filled with rocks from Lake Erie that are heated by a hellfire.

Hand railings help you climb. The higher you go, the hotter it is. This is not the sweet heat of the sauna. This is a heat so intense and focused it makes you supplicant. It bows your head and bends your knees. The slabs of baking flesh in here don't pass the time reading the Wall Street Journal. What they do, every couple of minutes, is empty five-gallon buckets of ice water over their heads, and that makes you wish you had brought a camera, but two minutes later you're doing the same thing.

In Today's High-Tech, High-Stress, Macho-Man World, There's Nothing Quite Like A Good Schvitz

••••

At the far end of the bleachers, a soapy, soaked towel lies on the top step. On the step below is a plastic bucket brimming with bubbles, a hose spilling cold water, and an old man in bathing trunks who performs the *platza*.

What that means is, he washes you with seaweed soaked in Ivory Snow, soaps you up into one big bubble, lightly rubbing and then slapping you, a cool towel over your head so you can breathe, whispering your name when it's time to turn over.

Once you are fully soaped, he helps you to your feet. The heat melts your bones like butter. You feel lightheaded, and all wet and mushy inside. You look ridiculous but nobody notices, they're too busy emptying buckets of ice water over their scorched skin, and you head down the bleachers and out of the *schvitz* and into the shower where the water can't get cold enough, fast enough.

When you have washed the soap off and you have stopped hyperventilating, you walk over to the far corner of the shower room where a low wall hides a dark blue ice-water pool. In the winter the water temperature stays about 40 degrees Fahrenheit. This time of year, August, the water is almost hot, nudging 60 degrees.

You dive in and if your heart doesn't explode, you are swept up in a rush of well-being and cleanliness that makes many men scream.

Now you are ready to eat. You dry yourself off and wrap the bedsheet around you like a toga. Then you go into the kitchen and select what you want to drink from a cooler full of pop and beer.

The only people you see with clothes on are the men in the kitchen. They take your order. Which is simple. All they serve is rib steak, cut fresh off the bone. Flame broiled. Coated in fresh, diced garlic. You just tell them how thick you want it.

The dining room sits under the watchful eye of Moshe Dayan. Men, attired in sheets and towels, eat alone or in small groups at the different tables. Some drink from bottles they brought. Most of them are older, and they argue about sports. A neon sign that reads "Fantasy Room" perches unplugged on a table in the corner. From the cots comes the sound of great snoring.

While you wait for the steak, you crunch chilled pickled sweet peppers and hot peppers and dill pickles. The salad is lettuce and tomato and onion, and the only dressing is oil and vinegar. The rye bread is crusty and fresh.

Whatever the heat didn't crush or the cold water shock or the rubdown relax or the *platza* wash away, the steak sedates.

You are dreamy-eyed and goofy, quite at home in your billowing bedsheet. It takes a long time to get dressed. You settle your bill, tallied on the honor system, in cash, as you walk out the door. It usually runs about $40 plus tip. Then you drift home, talking about things like why they picked Ivory Snow over, say, Palmolive. ■

Christopher Evans is a staff writer for the Magazine.

THE PLAIN DEALER MAGAZINE 38 SUNDAY, SEPTEMBER 16 1990

A 1990 story by Christopher Evans for the *Sunday Magazine* in the *Plain Dealer*. Evans's first experience at the Schvitz is crammed with quippy anecdotes, one of them being "This is not the sweet heat of the sauna. This is a heat so intense and focused it makes you supplicant." *Courtesy of the* Plain Dealer.

Perhaps Christopher Evans, who wrote an article about his first experience at the Schvitz for the *Plain Dealer Sunday Magazine* in September 1990, said it best: "This is not the sweet heat of the sauna....This heat melts your bones like butter." One wonders if that quote should be etched in stone above the wooden door leading into the steam room.

Fifteen years later, in another *Plain Dealer* article, writer Robert Smith emphasized Evans's experience: "Heat whooshed out as if from the throat of a volcano."

For Billy, he has fun with Schvitz newcomers when he walks into the steam room and they probe him with questions about the heat. "If it's someone new, I'll joke around that they're only ready for a 100-level course on the Schvitz heat," he laughs. Two of Billy's favorite go-to lines are "Schvitz Thermal Dynamics" and "Schvitz Physiology." Unfortunately, neither is offered at nearby Case Western or John Carroll University.

The steam at the Schvitz is one-of-a-kind and the last of its kind. It's grandfathered steam—meaning today it's illegal to make steam the way the Schvitz makes it. The building has been operating for so long that it predates many zoning laws and building code requirements.

The best way to describe the process of the Schvitz steam probably comes from Smith's *Plain Dealer* article from 2005. Considering the Schvitz never wanted to make front-page news, it's ironic that Smith's article,

ONLINE: WWW.CLEVELAND.COM

$1.50

PLAIN DEALER SUNDAY

SPORTS
DiMarco holds lead at Masters
LeBron scores 40 as Cavaliers beat Bucks, 98-81
TIGERS 11
INDIANS 1

Loung Ung seeks end to land mines
SUNDAY MAGAZINE

MORE THAN $330 IN COUPONS INSIDE

Detroit casinos bring in cash

But as Cleveland weighs gambling, Michigan finds bet hasn't solved city's woes

Cleveland Hts. band goes on the road
METRO

Porn plugs into new technologies
PDQ

What happens when Wal-Mart moves in
BUSINESS

A ROYAL WEDDING — THE SECOND TIME AROUND

Working up some steam for relaxation

Old-world Jewish tradition lives on at East Side's Schvitz

Religion, politics mix more than ever

GENERATION IN TROUBLE

Caring for the fallen, comforting the bereaved

This grandmother is called to the front lines in urban war

About this series

INSIDE

This page: A 2005 story by Robert Smith for the *Plain Dealer* detailing how the steam room works. It also states, "Newcomers must arrive with a regular customer," as was the preference of owner Mark Balogh, who in the same article said he had "the biggest, driest, hottest box in town." *Courtesy of the* Plain Dealer.

*A2 The Plain Dealer | Sunday, April 10, 2005

"You come here, the worries of the world drain away. Wives can't complain. It's all wholesome. It's the ultimate male bonding experience."

Victor Finamore, *a home builder from Munson Township*

SCHVITZ

FROM A1

Working up steam for relaxation

But among hundreds of men in Greater Cleveland, especially older Jewish men, you need only say "Let's meet at the Schvitz," and they begin to happily sweat. Just as their fathers did.

Public baths scrubbed the citizenry of teeming immigrant cities like Cleveland in the early 1900s, when hot water was a luxury. But a steam was always more than a bath in Jewish neighborhoods.

Jewish immigrants from Eastern Europe and Russia hailed from a steam-bath tradition. Their faith in the cleansing powers of super-hot baths took on new meaning in a new world.

To schvitz, the Yiddish word for sweat, came to mean to indulge in something satisfying and manly.

Maury Feren, 89, was a boy when his Russian immigrant father began taking him to "the old Schvitz," as he calls it, often on Friday afternoons before the Sabbath. Later, as a produce salesman, Feren took his clients to the Schvitz in the 1950s and '60s.

He still recalls the muscled arms of the man who applied the *platza* ("PLATE-zza"), a sudsy scrubbing with an oak-leaf broom. "He'd pour cold water over himself so he could stand the heat and take man after man, and he would be drinking whiskey," he said.

Times change. But not so much.

You can still get a *platza* at the old Schvitz, properly titled the Mount Pleasant Russian-Turkish Baths. Alan, the *parchik*, does not gulp whiskey after he whacks you on the back with a *bazem*. But he does lather up customers with artful intensity in a steam room virtually unchanged since 1927, when it opened.

A 1992 fire took a bite out of the Schvitz, but the spa survived and so did its tradition-soaked routines.

Upstairs, on the second floor, men still sit down to steak and herring dinners wearing only bedsheets. They nap in a dim room that resembles a M.A.S.H. unit with its twin rows of steel cots, and pay extra for pummeling massages called rubdowns.

In the soft sweaty din of the Schvitz, you can almost hear Tevye the [illegible]

Except that today, Tevye is likely to be a non-Jewish banker, even a priest. A venerable sauna survives by attracting a modern man.

On a recent Monday night, Victor Finamore, a home builder from Munson Township, walked into the 30-seat dining room and yelled hello to Joseph Myers, an architect from Kirtland Hills. They spread blueprints on a tabletop and filled glasses with red wine.

Six or seven friends would soon be joining them for the bimonthly guys night out.

Nearby, a broiler flamed and a band saw whirred. Steaks are cut from the bone in a small kitchen and served coated in garlic. The beer is cold and the cigars are fat.

"You come here, the worries of the world drain away," said Finamore, 47. "Wives can't complain. It's all wholesome. It's the ultimate male bonding experience."

He discovered the Schvitz the way most men do, with a tip from a friend. The Schvitz is pay-as-you-go — about $50 for a steam and a steak — and there are no dues. But newcomers must arrive with a regular customer.

Mark Balogh said word of mouth is all he needs. He's got the biggest, driest, hottest box in town. A former software salesman, Balogh came home from California in the early '90s to run the Schvitz for his friend Gay "Gabriel" Gold, who had inherited the business from his father.

Eight years ago, Balogh said, he and his brother, Greg, bought the Schvitz from Gold's widow, becoming its first non-Jewish owners. At the time, the Schvitz was experiencing a bit of a renaissance, which it needed.

Wednesday ladies nights died in the late 1960s because the neighborhood's Eastern European women had all moved away. The men left, too, and some were not coming back to the Schvitz.

A pair of coincidences helped to freshen the ranks of schvitzers.

Immigrants from the former Soviet Union, who streamed into the region in the '90s, soon discovered a sauna that felt like home. About the same time, a new, often non-Jewish generation of professional men took to the schvitz experience.

Joseph Lesco, an engineer and builder from University Heights, golfs at Acacia Country Club but said he relaxes more at the Schvitz, a place of simple protocol and little pretense.

All men stand equal in a towel and a bedsheet, he notes.

Dean Gladden, managing director of the Cleveland Play House, an Episcopalian and a regular schvitzer, likes the leisurely dinners, the debate and good cheer in a setting devoid of television.

"This is all about good conversation," he said.

Some talk fondly of the days when Murray Hill wiseguys mixed with rabbis, bookies and prosecutors in comfortable nudity, but regulars say some of the old flavor remains. Many a father still brings his son to the Schvitz as a rite of passage, often following a bar mitzvah. Colorful characters, from bikers to West Siders, don the bedsheet. And deals are still sealed on the steamy steps of the sauna.

Alan the *platza*-giver, who does not want his last name divulged, recalls the instructions that Gay Gold issued on his first day of work 23 years ago, words he said he still works by:

"Whatever you hear, whatever you see, stays right here," he was told. "Nothing leaves the Schvitz."

To reach this Plain Dealer reporter:
rsmith@plaind.com, 216-999-4024

Hot rocks, cold pool, Cleveland tradition

A public bath called a "schvitz" — the Yiddish word for sweat — still exists in Cleveland, though few are left in the United States. In the early 20th century, immigrants from eastern Europe and Russia used them to cleanse, relax and socialize. The steam room gets its heat from a 78-year-old sauna system. Here's how it works:

"Working Up Some Steam for Relaxation: Old-World Jewish Tradition Lives On at East Side's Schvitz," made it to the front page. Here's a quick, 100-level description of how the steam works:

> *A gas-powered oven heats granite rocks for 6–8 hours.*
>
> *As the oven heats up, the rocks expand, trapping the heat.*
>
> *At a spigot near the oven, men fill buckets with hot water and heave the water into the oven, on the rocks.*
>
> *When water hits the hot rocks, the water relieves the pressure of the rocks. As the rocks shrink back down, supercharged steam escapes the oven and vaporizes, making a hissing sound.*

A couple other items of note: According to the article, the oven walls are thirty inches thick. Moisture in the air hovers around 20 percent, leaning more toward a dry sauna than a humid steam room. Cured cypress and cedar bleachers are less prone to warp and rot in a humid environment.

"It Was Like Touching the Sun"

"About five years ago, this very loud and boisterous guy who comes every year damn near killed everyone in the steam room," says Ryan Supler of University Heights.

> *In the steam room, there is a special metal bucket that you fill with hot water to throw into the oven to get it steamy. You don't do it often, otherwise it gets unbearably hot.*
>
> *Anyway, the bucket has holes drilled about two inches up so that you can only fill so much water before you throw it in. Well, crazy man decides to fill up one of the five-gallon buckets on the bleachers. These buckets are supposed to be used to cool yourself off, not to fill and throw into the oven. He filled up the five-gallon bucket and threw all the water into the oven.*
>
> *I have never seen or heard something like it before. Steam flew out of the oven, audibly and visually. You could see the heatwaves (imagine like a black top in a desert, with the wavy lines), and everyone just kind of had this "Oh shit" expression.*
>
> *The steam flies out, hits the top corner and starts moving to the side. Dudes were cannonballing off the top two rows, like reckless throwing*

themselves off. My friend Steve was near that top corner where it gets hottest first, and he legit had bubbling skin on his shoulder and side. It usually runs about 200 to 220 on the thermometer on the top row. I imagine it had to have shot up to 300 degrees instantly. I can't confirm actual numbers, but it was like touching the sun.

The entire place cleared out, fast. We had to keep the door open for like fifteen minutes just to cool it down, and it was still unbearable for almost an hour. It was wild and was a quick lesson for everyone.

Anyway, as a physical therapist, one time I had this cardiovascular doctor, and I'm working him and I'm like "Hey man, you look familiar," and we kept talking, and I couldn't figure out where. Next time I see him, I'm like "Hey, random question, have you ever been to the Schvitz?" and he is like "OMG I love that place!" so we get to talking and realize we've been at the party together before, and then it dawns on me.

I'm like "Wait, one last question: are you the guy that almost killed everyone by throwing the five-gallon bucket on it?" and he is like "Oh shit, you remember! I will never live that down! I have never felt that bad in my life. I think I burned some guys!" We had some good laughs over our next few visits.

Branch Beatings

If the Schvitz were Red Lobster, the *platza* would be the cheddar bay biscuits—not the main course but a savory part of the whole experience. Here is the platza description from russianandturkishbaths.com:

A Platza (Yiddish for shoulders or back) is a potent Russian healing tool enjoyed in an inferno of a room known as a Schvitz or Banya. This is a traditional Russian experience unlike any other.

It is done on the uppermost bench, because heat rises, with an oak leaf broom called a venik, a very leafy, fragrant bundle of extremely fresh oak tree twigs. The fresh forest-like smell of the venik creates a sedative effect and melts stress. The venik leaves release organic phytoncides and infection inhibitors, decreasing the growth and development of pathogens in the body. Essential oils are also released, preventing premature aging of the skin. The oak leaves contain a natural astringent, which will open your pores, remove toxins, and exfoliate dead skin. Steam bathing stimulates protein

> *circulation while improving digestibility of proteins, fats, carbohydrates, and mineral elements. This intensifies skin capillary activities and strengthens metabolism as the body is filled with energy and the immune system is improved.*

As mentioned in the introduction, Billy has been giving platzas for decades. If you tell a Schvitz veteran you're going to the Schvitz for the first time, they'll tell you to get a platza, the same way they'd tell you to get a corned beef sandwich at Slyman's.

When *With Light Steam* author Bryon MacWilliams visited the Schvitz back in 2017, he was impressed with Billy's resilience and stamina. "When I saw Billy in the steam room, it was clear he was in good banya shape. Being at the top bench is hot enough, but when you're moving around and scrubbing people down, it can be laboring. I could tell he had been doing it a long time."

In MacWilliams's book he offers this Russian proverb: "'Happy, as if fresh from the banya.' The saying is accurate, and reflects the physical bliss a person with a clean, scrubbed body experiences."

Mark Cousineau from Shaker Heights says:

> *I was always curious about the platza. I had seen guys getting whipped with branches in the sauna before, so I decided to try it for myself. As I lay on my stomach on the top bench, the platza guy washed me with a soft, soapy sponge. Then he followed it up by scrubbing me with a rougher sponge, which felt gritty but great at the same time. Finally, he whipped me with the branches, which smelled like eucalyptus. Amazing!*

Cousineau also recalls a heart-skipping moment involving the platza. "Before I had ever gotten a platza, a buddy of mine whipped me on the back and sides with the branches as we were steaming"—the equivalent of guys in high school snapping each other with towels.

"When I went to the bathroom, I looked down, and my dick was black!" As time froze for a second, Cousineau reached down and removed the wet black substance from his crotch. It was a leaf from one of the branches.

Pummeling Pleasure

Every nickname bestowed upon somebody has a great backstory. This is the case with Kevin "Noodles" Lynch. Lynch grew up in Euclid and was first exposed to the Schvitz when he was nineteen.

"My older brother told me he was taking me to a nice steak dinner place for my birthday. When we got there, I had no idea what the hell was going on," Lynch fondly recalls.

Lynch's experience is typical in the sensory whirlwind overload that is the Schvitz. Is this place like a gym or a low-class country club? Perhaps a secret urban oasis? Why is everyone in towels?

Eventually, Kevin's older brother got him acquainted with the locker room setup and the dining room. The two, along with some friends, headed down into the steam room. Lynch, being very green both in life experience and Schvitz customs, listened intently as his brother explained how the steam room worked.

"My brother told me to go ahead and throw some water in the oven. At the time I didn't know they were setting me up!" Only about thirty minutes into his Schvitz experience, Lynch threw a bucket of water in the oven. That's when things got interesting.

At the time in 1999, Billy Buckholtz's uncle Alan Buckholtz worked at the Schvitz and was known as a bit of a curmudgeon. He walked around with an irritable demeanor, especially to those Schvitz newbies who didn't get how it all went down.

How it worked was Alan was the *only* person allowed to throw water in the oven. In Russia, Alan's position is referred to as *banshchik*, or "bath superintendent." As the story is told, Alan happened to be outside the steam room when he heard the familiar hiss of the water hitting the rocks. *Hisssssssssss*.

Alan, who was older and not necessarily quick on his feet, burst into the steam room and demanded to know the culprit. "Who the fuck threw water in my oven? Who the fuck was it?!" Kevin, terrified of the crime he didn't know he committed, stayed silent until Alan left the steam room in disgust. Kevin's heart sank.

"I wasn't necessarily intimidated—I wrestled in high school—but more ashamed of what I had done," recalls Lynch. He headed upstairs and put himself in a self-imposed timeout to think about what he had done. About thirty minutes later, Alan came upstairs to let the youngster know everything was OK.

"He came up to me and said, 'Hey, sorry I got so worked up. I didn't know the guys had goaded you into it. It's OK; around here I control the steam, but we're all good.'"

After exhaling, Kevin enjoyed the rest of his first Schvitz experience. When he got back to the parking lot, he asked his brother and his friends, "So, when are we coming back?"

Fast-forward two years later to 2001. Kevin, now trained in Thai massage, was invited by Mark and Greg Balogh to be the third masseur on staff. "I had come to the Schvitz a ton after that first baptism by fire, and Mark and Greg knew I was going to massage school. They always said I should come work there when I was done with my training, and sure enough, I did."

When Kevin started, the main masseur at the Schvitz was a big, burly Russian named Boris—stereotypes be damned! "I believe Boris was in the Russian army when he was younger and later went on to become a doctor or some other esteemed healthcare professional in his native country," says Lynch. "Since sometimes the degrees or credentials don't carry over into the States, he found work in the States as a masseur. I think he had an Osteo-type background; he could crunch bones with his adjustments."

Steve Presser, former owner of Big Fun on Coventry Road in Cleveland Heights, remembers Boris well. "Oh man, do I remember those massages. Boris would ask me what kind of massage I wanted [impersonating a heavy Russian accent], 'American or KGB?' I always opted for somewhere in the middle," Presser laughs.

When Boris retired, one of his frequent Schvitz clients came in eager to get a massage. Mark told the man a new masseur named Kevin would be working on him since Boris had left. The man took a look at Kevin, who was about 160 pounds soaking wet, and remarked that the new massage kid looked "skinny and wiry." He also questioned Kevin's strength to provide a deep-tissue massage. Challenge accepted.

After the man got his massage, he staggered out and told Mark Balogh, "That kid worked me. I feel like a wet noodle." In an ironic coincidence, Kevin's family had owned TeaHouse Noodles on East 6th in Cleveland for nearly twenty-five years (1995–2018). Now and then, Kevin would bring Thai noodles for the staff, and Mark and Greg would occasionally remark, "Thanks, Noodles."

When the gentleman said he felt like a wet noodle after Kevin's massage, Mark couldn't help himself. Kevin recalls, "When I walked into the kitchen, Mark said, 'Hey, that guy you just worked on. He said you made him feel like a wet noodle, Noodles.' That's when the name stuck."

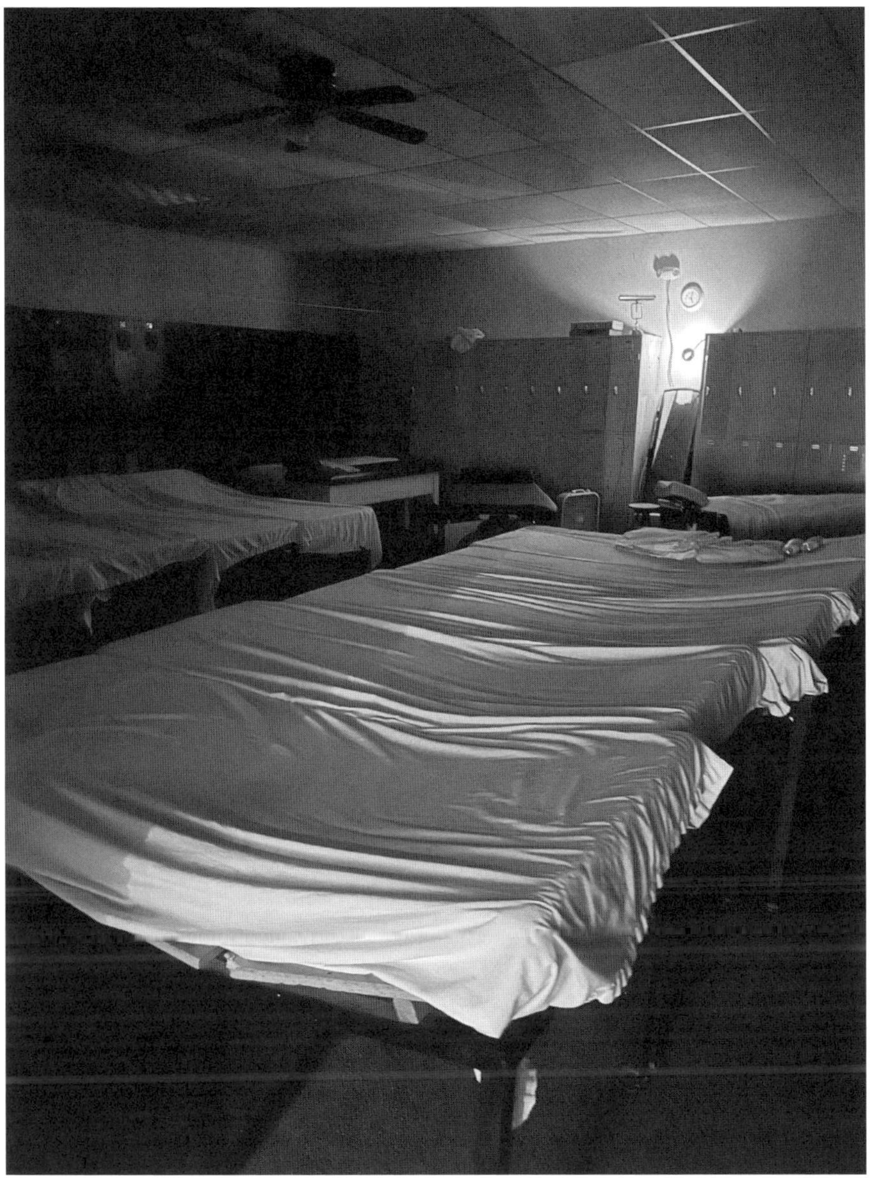

The cots are lined up ready for massages. The locker room of the Schvitz, which doubles as the massage parlor, has been described as part old-school boxing gym and part *M*A*S*H* triage unit. *Courtesy of Jason Morris.*

Funny nicknames aside, Lynch recognized even at an early age what an important job he had as a young masseur. "Touch is the last sense to go," says Lynch. "It's a way to still feel connected to other human beings, and serious Schvitz guys appreciate that."

Cold Plunging Before It Was Cool

When most people think of the Schvitz or "schvitzing," they think only of the heat—guys in towels or less sitting, sweating and telling stories. But if you ask any Schvitz purists, the cold plunge pool is the yin-yang of the whole experience.

About twenty feet away from the steam room lies a mini pool with water anywhere from forty-five to sixty-five degrees. If you're brave enough, you'll expose yourself to extreme cold after extreme heat. At the Schvitz, everything is kind of extreme. But here's the kicker: shocking your body between hot and cold environments is one of the healthiest things you can do.

In *Sweat: Uncovering Your Body's Hidden Superpower*, Justin Glaser uncovers a story about blacksmith William Bratton, a member of the Lewis and Clark Expedition. In 1806, Bratton was ailed by debilitating lower back pain and weakness, making it difficult to walk or even sit. John Shields, who acted as the principal blacksmith for the expedition, suggested an out-of-the-box remedy.

A four-foot hole was dug, and at the bottom of the hole, stones were heated by fire. Bratton sat naked on a seat above the scalding stones, and water was sprinkled on the stones to produce steam. A makeshift tent made of willow poles and blankets kept the heat in.

Bratton braved the heat and was then lifted out of the seat by members of the expedition. His body was plunged into a nearby cold river. This cycle of stone-induced heat and chilly river water was repeated twice.

The next day, Bratton was able to move freely without pain. Bratton's ailment was believed to be a mix of degenerative disc disease and arthritis. The heat and cold provided a potent cure.

In just the past few years, cold plunging, or cold therapy, has taken the world by storm. Wim Hof, a Dutch extreme athlete known as "The Iceman," now in his sixties, has helped put cold therapy on the map with his feats of cold exposure. He holds the very niche Guinness World Record for fastest half-marathon run while barefoot on ice or snow, clocking in at 2:16:34. Hof's cold therapy combines cold exposure, meditation and breathwork.

Even more recently, Gary Brecka, a human biologist and health influencer with close to two million Instagram followers, has helped bring cold therapy into the mainstream. Brecka used to work in the life insurance industry and claims he could predict down to the month when someone would pass away as a result of their bloodwork.

The science is still developing on cold plunging, but at a glance, here are key benefits described by Elise Free, owner of Elemental Wellness in Westlake, Ohio. "Lower inflammation, a spark in metabolism, and a resetting of the nervous system are the most immediate benefits," says Free. "There's a beautiful pharmacy within our own body, and healthy stressors like ice baths and saunas are great healers."

The word *pharmacy* struck a chord with me. In Katja Pantzar's enlightening book *The Finnish Way*, she describes saunas and steam rooms as a "poor man's pharmacy." What does this mean? From my standpoint, it means frequent, controlled healthy stressors like heat and cold have healing effects you can't measure in milligrams.

Brecka describes aging as the "aggressive pursuit of comfort." He's right. Most of us have conditioned our lives like Goldilocks—not too hot or too cold. "The mind-body connection is very real," Free goes on. "Our body stores trauma, and sometimes we don't know how to get out of our way."

From firsthand experience, I can tell you that Free is spot-on. I joined a few members of Elemental Wellness in February 2024 for a cold plunge in Lake Erie. The water was thirty-six degrees, and it hurt, like knives poking into your skin. But afterward, all—and I mean all—the inflammation in my body was shocked out of my system.

Free appreciates what the Schvitz offers, a place where healthy stressors restore your mind and body by heating up and cooling down. "The Schvitz is doing a great job of what I'm trying to create at Elemental Wellness. A community that thrives on hot and cold."

Chapter 7

WHY IS THE FOOD (ESPECIALLY THE STEAK) SO GOOD AT THE SCHVITZ?

The steam and steak are the 1A and 1B of the Schvitz experience. You can't talk about the steam without talking about the steak. And if you ask loyal Schvitz-goers, places like Morton's and Hyde Park are just pretenders to the throne.

When I posted in Facebook groups about the writing of this book, most of the comments were about the food, and the steak in particular. In Irv Siedman's essay "Going to the Schvitz" found on ClevelandJewishHistory.net, he mentions the steak: "Although now I am a vegetarian who eats fish, I think one piece of meat I might eat again is a steak covered in grilled garlic at the schvitz."

Similarly, Doug Trattner's article from *Cleveland SCENE* in 2011 echoes the same feeling: "It might be the heat stroke and Heineken talking, but steak just doesn't get better than this."

"On a good night, they'll go through one or two cows, literally," says Andrew Zuccaro. "I usually smell like garlic for a few days after, but it's worth it." Andrew is right. I probably should've made the pages of this book a scratch and sniff of cloved garlic.

"The garlic smell is pungent," says Jim Sollisch of Cleveland Heights. "My first wife hated when I came home from the Schvitz, smelling of garlic. She would make me sleep on the couch. When I was dating my second wife, I came home from the Schvitz, again, smelling like garlic, but she didn't bat an eye and greeted me with a hug and a kiss. I knew that was a good sign." Jim and his second wife are still married.

Jerry Weinzimmer, owner of WW Meats, the original supplier of meats for the Schvitz and other notable Cleveland restaurants. *Courtesy of Billy Buckholtz.*

One person who knows the food well at the Schvitz is Paul Fierman, who joined the Schvitz as a chef in 2022. "I showed up to interview with Billy in a suit and fedora hat," Fierman recalls. "I should've shown up in what I usually wear in the kitchen: jeans and a T-shirt."

Fierman, dressed to the nines with resume in hand, is a kitchen lifer who's been and cooked everywhere. He graduated with a degree in hospitality management and culinary arts from Cuyahoga Community College. He also has an associate's degree in applied business, along with certificates of proficiency in professional baking and professional culinarian, along with completion of ServSafe® programs such as food handler and food protection manager.

Most of the places Fierman has cooked at are familiar—chains like Olive Garden, Chipotle and Fuddruckers. But the ironic part is his experience cooking for the Jewish community in various synagogues in the Cleveland area. As mentioned earlier, the Schvitz building was a synagogue before it became a bathhouse.

Fierman caught on quickly. He was firing up steaks in no time but also realized the Schvitz catered to more than just carnivores. "Obviously we are known for the steaks, but we take pride in everything we serve," said Fierman.

The Schvitz has seen an uptick in guests opting for the salmon, tuna or vegetarian options as more people get health conscious. "We want people to feel comfortable in whatever their dietary habits are. Billy wants it to be enjoyable for everyone. It doesn't matter if you're vegetarian or kosher or whatever; we'll cook it up for you the right way," says Fierman.

The relationship between the customers and the chefs is another interesting part of the Schvitz experience. When a regular walks in, he'll sometimes be greeted with a jolly "Where the fuck have you been?!" from one of the kitchen staff. Steaks are served with a heavy side of ball-busting.

Though the ball-busting can be relentless, with it comes a certain respect and care for your fellow man.

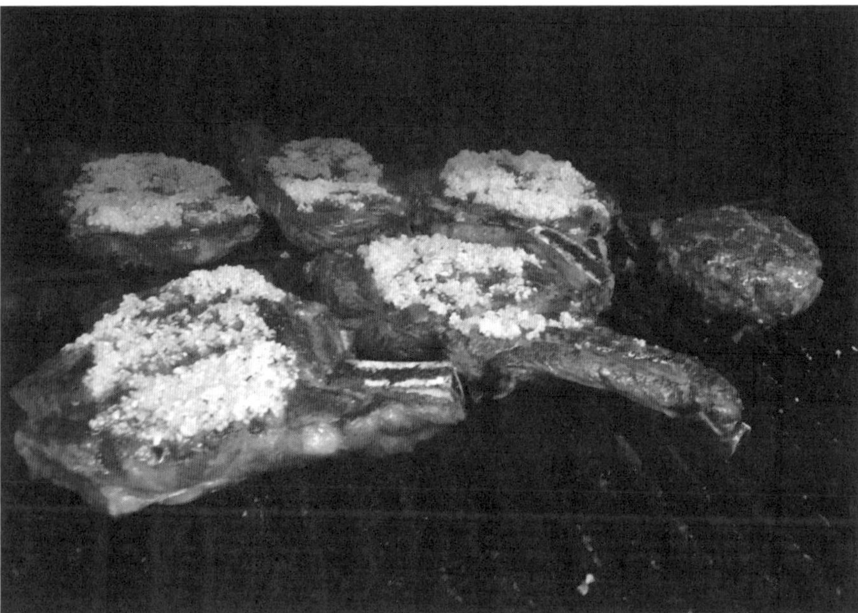

Top: A stack of steaks from Blue Ribbon Meats. As Andrew Zuccaro said, "On a good night, they'll go through one or two cows, literally." *Courtesy of Paul Fierman.*

Bottom: Steaks smothered in cloved garlic. It stings the nostrils. The burger, also made from steak trimmings, is a fan favorite. A Schvitz steak is not unlike a Polish Boy or a corned b eef sandwich from Slyman's—Cleveland traditions that must be tried at least once. *Courtesy of Paul Fierman.*

"One time a couple years back I was having a rough day," says Fierman. "My wife and kid got in a car accident, and my son had internal bleeding from the crash. My mind was scattered, and I guess I was wearing the heaviness on my face.

"Al Mancuso, a regular, could sense something was up. He pulled me aside and asked if I was OK, and I explained what happened. That one-on-one time meant a lot to me, the sense that he could pick up on my mood."

Schvitz staff worker Stevie cutting meat on the famous bandsaw. *Courtesy of Billy Buckholtz.*

Fierman enjoys the relationships he's made at the Schvitz, with both staff and guests. "Billy is a rock star, literally!" says Fierman. "If I had some extra cash, I'd invest in the place. I hope to be here for a long time."

Steakhouse Attire

Steve Presser recalls a funny story where the term "steakhouse" was misinterpreted.

"I decided to do our holiday party for Big Fun employees at the Schvitz; this was sometime in the early '90s," says Presser. "I had a young kid working for me, Troy, who was about eighteen. I got a call from his mother. She said, 'Troy told me you were doing a steakhouse for the company Christmas party. That's so nice! I want to make sure he's dressed accordingly. What should he wear?'"

Before unleashing his quick wit with a retort like, "Uh, a towel," or "Just come naked," Presser explained to Troy's mother that they were going to the Schvitz. His mother, from the area and familiar with the establishment, laughed with Presser when she learned of this so-called steakhouse.

Sharing Is Caring

One of the unwritten rules of the Schvitz is a notion most of us learned in elementary school, and that's to make sure you bring enough for the whole class.

The Schvitz is unique in that it encourages you to bring your own appetizers and drinks to heighten the experience. There's a potluck element to the food on the tables, everything from charcuterie boards to shrimp to chips and cookies and more. It's long been a Schvitz tradition to bring some of your raw meats as well. And as long as you ask nicely, the Schvitz will happily cook sausages, shrimp, clams and so on. A restaurant that lets you bring in appetizers and alcohol! Try doing that at Mabel's or Blue Point Grille, in nothing but a towel no less.

"The amount of booze and wine at any table could feed a large Italian family at Thanksgiving," says Eric Mack of University Heights. As part of the fraternal nature of food sharing that takes place, many experience certain drinks and delicacies for the very first time.

"I consider myself pretty low on the Schvitz totem pole, earnings wise," laughs Alan Mancuso, who's been coming since 2001. "I was a seafood salesman, then a water meter reader and now I'm a health inspector for the city [Cleveland]. I know the Schvitz is the great equalizer in that everyone is just there to relax and let their guard down, but certain pleasures are just out of my price range."

One time when Mancuso was in the dining room, he struck up a conversation with a gentleman who happily offered him a glass of whiskey. But it wasn't just any whiskey.

"He poured me a generous glass of a twenty-five-year-old Macallan [a single-malt scotch whiskey]. A bottle of it goes for over $2,000! Man, that went down smooth."

Another Schvitz veteran, Ryan Supler, has a similar story. "One time this older guy brought like a hundred mini-bottles of different scotches. It was cool as hell!" recalls Supler. "A ton of different varieties, years, brands, etc. He would be like, 'Oh, you'll love this '76' and give me a pour of it. A serious scotch man."

Kevin Lynch laughs about the education he got on food and wine at the Schvitz. "The Schvitz is where I learned what good wine and good scotch were. The pairings were important, too, like what fine cheeses go best with certain wines. But it spoiled me! Now my tastes are so expensive thanks to all the great stuff those guys brought in," Lynch fondly remembers.

Chef's Kiss

"If you can't have a good time at the Schvitz, you've got serious issues," says Fahrenheit owner and chef Rocco Whalen. "The Schvitz has quality food and thoughtful side dishes. And the camaraderie can't be beat."

Whalen knows a thing or two about food. In 2002, he opened Fahrenheit in Tremont, just minutes away from downtown. The restaurant quickly gained local and national attention, in large part due to Whalen's prowess not just in the kitchen but in his overall management of food and hospitality. He's accomplished, to say the least, and if you ask him where one of the best places in Cleveland is to eat and relax, the Schvitz will inevitably come up.

"Back in the day, a lot of the old Tremont crew would go there, guys like me and Michael Symon. Jonathon Sawyer would come, too. We would book it over to Luke Avenue and be there in ten minutes."

The endorsement of Whalen and other respected Northeast Ohio chefs is an important one. They are the rock stars of Cleveland. Could you recognize the councilman who runs your ward? Or the police or fire chief? Maybe, but probably not. Cleveland has quietly gained a reputation as a foodie city, and many of those responsible for the surge in popularity love to get their steam on.

"It's just such a great place to relax," says Whalen. "A group of us would get there early, like twelve or one, and stay until three or four and then head straight to our restaurants to cook. You never knew what interesting foods people would bring. Grandma's cookies, clams—you sampled everything."

As a fellow businessman, Whalen is both fascinated by and supportive of what Billy has done. "I think the business model is great—mostly cash. They have the usual expenses like food, water, staff, electricity and all that, but it's very lean."

And as far as the $150 price tag that goes with the Schvitz, Whalen doesn't blink an eye. "Things aren't cheap anymore, and it's a free enterprise," says Whalen. "If someone has a problem with the cost then they shouldn't be there in the first place."

Chapter 8

I HEARD THE SCHVITZ CAUGHT ON FIRE. IS THAT TRUE?

"Ryan started the fire!" Sorry, I had a quote from *The Office* in my last book and felt like this one needed one, too. Back to the story.

The Schvitz caught fire (not from Ryan) on March 28, 1992. Records show the Cleveland Fire Department got the call a little before 6:00 p.m., and the fire was contained by 7:28 p.m., taking fifty firefighters to put out the blaze. In an article from the *Plain Dealer*, acting Assistant Fire Chief Paul J. Marks estimated the damage to be around $100,000. The fire was contained when firefighters found a fire escape that accessed the second-floor storage area.

Like the Schvitz itself, the story of the fire is one shrouded in mystery. Was it planned? Was it retribution for something? Or was it just an accident?

A WEWS-TV5 report stated that "the building had been abandoned for years and was believed to be a bathhouse at one time." To be fair, the Schvitz does have that charming abandoned look you just can't find on HGTV. More importantly, the news report demonstrated just how secluded the Schvitz had been. Those who went there knew what it was all about. Obviously WEWS-TV5 hadn't had a good sweat and steak in a while, or ever. Cleveland, in a sense, had forgotten about the Schvitz. The same report mentioned the fire department believed it could be arson.

"No, it wasn't arson; it was an accident," says Darcy Desatnik of Mayfield Heights. Desatnik is the daughter of Gay Gold, who owned the Schvitz at the time of the fire. "At the time, the building was getting some plumbing work done from Ernie Fisco, who ran Triple A Plumbing, and one of the pipes had a gas leak somewhere. But since there was no insurance, a cause was never determined."

Fire damages bathhouse

CLEVELAND

An East Side bathhouse that has been a Cleveland institution since the 1920s was hit by fire yesterday, sustaining an estimated $100,000 damage.

Officials did not have a name for the bathhouse, which is on Luke Ave. off E. 116th St., but it has been referred to simply as the schvitz, which is Yiddish for steam bath.

The fire destroyed the one-story restaurant portion of the building, but the adjoining two-story bathhouse was saved.

Firefighters were called to the blaze shortly before 6 p.m. and it took 50 firefighters until 7:28 to bring it under control, fire officials said.

The cause of the fire had not been determined last night.

Acting Assistant Fire Chief Paul J. Marks, who estimated the damage, said firefighters used a fire escape to enter the second-floor storage area of the bathhouse to stop the fire from spreading there. The fire damaged only the roof of the bathhouse.

A manager told firefighters he had left about an hour before the fire was reported.

Bathhouse officials could not be reached for comment.

The bathhouse has shunned attention and draws its clientele largely by word of mouth.

JCPENNEY CORRECTION NOTICE

This week's 90th Anniversary circular contains the wrong starting date. This event begins Sunday, March 29.

We are sorry for any inconvenience this may have caused.

Left: A blurb after the 1992 fire. Highlights of the article include "The cause of the fire had not been determined" and "Bathhouse officials could not be reached for comment." *Courtesy of the* Plain Dealer.

Below: A postcard for the Schvitz during the Greg and Mark Balogh era. The picture shows the remnants of the fire with the quippy headline "Feeling a little burned out?" *Courtesy of Billy Buckholtz*.

Pictures from the fire in 1992. To illustrate how secretive the Schvitz was, a WEWS-TV5 report stated that "the building had been abandoned for years and was believed to be a bathhouse at one time." *Courtesy of Billy Buckholtz.*

Darcy's younger sister, Wendy Gold, remembers Fisco feeling awful about what happened. "As the firefighters were putting out the blaze, Ernie got wind of what happened and immediately drove up to the Schvitz. Someone says that they remember him crying in the parking lot."

At the time of the fire, Gay Gold was over seventy and had been battling prostate cancer for years. The prostate cancer eventually turned to bladder cancer, and Gay had to have his bladder removed. "My dad was slowing down a bit when the fire happened," says Desatnik.

Interesting, Powerful Friends of the Schvitz

Enter David "Doovy" Kirschenbaum. Kirschenbaum, who grew up in the Kinsman area as one of the "Kinsman Cowboys," went on to become an accomplished workmen's compensation attorney and also a real estate developer who owned nursing homes in Ohio and Arizona. With all the success though, he never forgot where he came from.

"My dad was an actualizer and synonymous with the Schvitz," says his daughter, Jo Kirschenbaum Cowan. "He always said, 'When God has been good to you, it's criminal not to share.'" For Doovy, the Schvitz fire was simply an inconvenience, not a problem. "My dad's attitude was there are no wrong turns, just new adventures."

David "Doovy" Kirschenbaum, who grew up in the Kinsman area, helped finance the Schvitz rebuild after the 1992 fire. Without him, there's a chance the Schvitz could have closed permanently or moved to a wealthier east side suburb. *Courtesy of Jo Kirschenbaum Cowan.*

By 1992 when the fire happened, the Kinsman area, where Kirschenbaum had enjoyed his vibrant youth, was a shadow of its former self, with many of the homes and buildings boarded up.

"I think my dad was getting a little burnt out," says Darcy of her father, Gay Gold. "Building a new Schvitz would've been starting over, and he was at the age and health where he didn't want the headache. He decided to work with what was left of the Schvitz from the fire."

Doovy understood Gay's view and immediately went to work finding contractors, painters and electricians to come in and get the place back up and running.

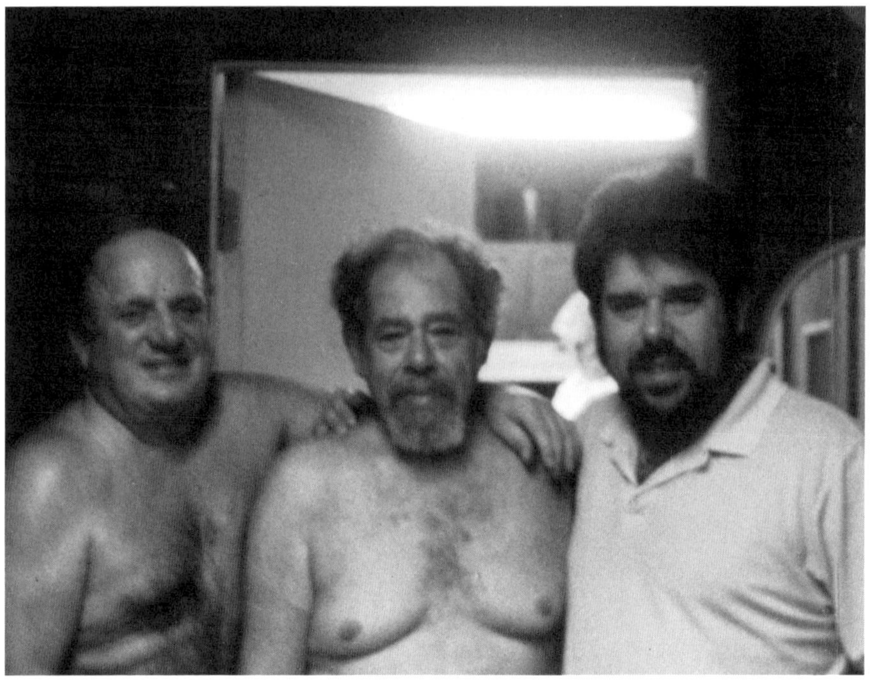

From left to right: David "Doovy" Kirschenbaum and Alan and Billy Buckholtz. *Courtesy of Billy Buckholtz.*

"My dad financed a lot of it himself," says Jo. "He had the respect of the guys in the neighborhood who went on to have blue-collar careers." Doovy was well connected. When he called, you picked up, and you said yes to the request.

Another key contributor to the Schvitz rebuild was a close friend of Gay Gold's, Roy Curtis. Curtis grew up in Lakewood and later made his money in manufacturing. A veteran who served in the U.S. Army, Curtis founded the Brite Metal Treating Company in Cleveland in 1961. Like Doovy, he had deep pockets and an affection for Gay and the Schvitz. Curtis also possessed some of those "most interesting man in the world" qualities that made him larger than life to those around him.

"I remember Roy taking me and my family on his private plane from Richmond Heights to Put-in-Bay," recalls Brant Desatnik. "I think I was about nine, and Roy let me 'fly' the plane (or made me believe I was flying it) as I sat on his lap in the cockpit."

Desatnik goes on: "I also remember he built a helicopter, and my grandpa would not let him take me for a ride because he was just learning how to fly it." Desatnik laughs. "About a week after that, he crashed it and it was totaled, but he lived!"

Kevin Lynch, who gave countless massages to Curtis in the early 2000s, remembers Curtis as a kind man of high integrity. "Roy was great, very nice, very inclusive," recalls Lynch. "When Roy got older and couldn't move around as well, I would drive to his place for massages. I don't do too many house calls, but Roy was a guy I liked and respected."

Kirschenbaum and Curtis no doubt had interesting hobbies and lives, but Eugene Phinick might have the most decorated story of them all.

Phinick is best remembered in the Cleveland area for owning Kronheim's, the popular Northeast Ohio furniture store. He and a group of investors purchased Kronheim's in 1963. But Phinick's life went way beyond selling furniture and enjoying the occasional steam.

Phinick led a very Forrest Gump–like life, serving in the Fifty-Fifth Armored Infantry Battalion in World War II and fighting in the Battle of the Bulge in Germany's Ardennes Forest. Like Gump, Phinick was shot by a sniper in the lower back while carrying a wounded soldier to safety. After recuperating, he reentered active duty and solidified his standing in U.S. and world history. The term "war hero" gets thrown around, but for Phinick, it might be an understatement.

In 1944, at not even twenty years old, Phinick and his squadron helped to liberate the Dachau and Mauthausen concentration camps. Phinick received two Purple Hearts, the Victory Medal, three bronze stars, citations for military bravery and the French Legion of Honor Medal, France's highest military distinction.

As for the fire, it marked a distinct fork in the road in how the Schvitz would continue. Would the fire be the end of its then almost seventy-year run? According to who you ask, Willy Kraus, a local attorney, advocated for a new, more modern Schvitz to be built on the east side in the Landerhaven development in Mayfield Heights. Kraus, a former lieutenant colonel in the army during World War II, was a power player in his own right and had gathered an unofficial board, with each member agreeing to contribute $50,000 to pay for the new Schvitz. Kraus was known to many as "Carnation Willie," as he was known for wearing a fresh flower in his lapel button daily.

Kirschenbaum, who everyone respected and more or less had the final say, thought about the proposal for a second but quickly decided to keep the Schvitz where it was. An anonymous source said, "Doovy told Krause and his board that Kinsman was where he grew up and that he felt strongly the Schvitz should remain there."

When I mentioned to Schvitzers the possibility of the Schvitz having moved, they wince. The Schvitz is synonymous with its surroundings, as part of the excitement is the drive there.

Michael DeAloia was the former CEO of Evergreen Podcasts and a former columnist at the *Plain Dealer*. He's also penned multiple books about Cleveland, including *Lost Cleveland: Seven Wonders of the Sixth City*.

"I was invited by a buddy of mine to go to the Schvitz, and as we made a left from Kinsman on East 116th, on the side of the road we saw a car on fire, just blazing," recalls DeAloia. After driving by and making sure nobody was still in the car, DeAloia couldn't help but laugh. "It just added to the whole experience."

As the Schvitz was being rebuilt, a small group of loyal patrons, mostly east-siders, got their steak and sweat fix out at "the farm." The farm was Doovy Kirschenbaum's sprawling multi-acre property in the affluent Cleveland suburb of Gates Mills. One of the features, in addition to a tennis court, in-ground outdoor pool and stable of horses, was a pool house that developed its own allure and stories.

"You never knew who would pop by," says Lynn Gross, Doovy's daughter, who still lives on the compound. "Some guys would come by at five or six in the morning to sweat. We jokingly called it 'Schvitz East.' Schvitz East is a traditional sauna located in the pool house that can seat four or five people. There's a small shower next to the sauna, along with a kitchen and a classic, Schvitz-like oven to fire up the steaks. It was the next best thing to being on Luke Avenue.

As mentioned in the introduction, as we get older, we forget a lot of things. But you'd be hard-pressed to meet someone who forgot their first time at the Schvitz.

"It wasn't until my early twenties that I got to go," says Gross. "I was going through a rough breakup with a boyfriend and was kind of depressed, just sort of in a fog. I think my dad was sick of me moping around and one day said, 'Let's go for a steak and a steam,' and half an hour later, we were at the Schvitz."

"I remember walking in and seeing this huge rat!" Gross laughs as she recalls. "I said, 'Gay, there's a huge rat over here!' Gay didn't seem too bothered and replied, 'Ah, don't worry, Smoky will get 'em.'" Smoky was a stray dog Gay had taken in.

One of the main features of the Schvitz that burned down was the hotel portion, or the "dormitories" as they were often called. The first ad for the Mount Pleasant Russian-Turkish Bathhouse in 1927 advertised a "Beautiful

Hotel with 30 Large Rooms." "Large" may have been an exaggeration, but the rooms are a fascinating part of the Schvitz's story, as not a lot of people remember them. There are stories of traveling salesmen staying in the rooms on their way to and from Chicago or patrons of the Schvitz who had too much to drink and simply slept in the rooms overnight.

"On Saturday nights, guys would show up around midnight to sweat the alcohol out and then go sleep in one of the rooms. Coming home sober Sunday morning was a better alternative than coming home drunk Saturday night and getting yelled at by your wife," says Marc Seigel.

Someone also suggested that it could have been a hideout for wiseguys, most notably Cleveland Mafia boss John Scalish, who grew up in the Kinsman area. One can't help but imagine if the Schvitz still had the dormitories today. Men might never leave the place! Or they would at least make a weekend out of it.

In a memory of eerie timing, Billy remembers the flames that fateful night in 1992. "My wife, Michele, and I were driving on the 480 bridge, going to meet friends for dinner, and I saw smoke in the distance. I didn't think anything of it."

When Billy got home, he had a frantic voicemail on his answering machine. "My dad left me a message and was practically in tears. He said, 'The Schvitz burned down! The Schvitz burned down!'"

The Schvitz was closed for close to a year. The frame building introduced as the hotel or the boardinghouse, the original kitchen, the dining hall and the locker room were all destroyed. But Billy prefers to look at the bright side of things: "Get this. The shower room, pool and steam room were untouched by the smoke and flames. All the tile, brick and marble slabs are exactly the same. Perhaps a miracle? Or just old-style construction with solid materials. Built to last!"

Chapter 9

DID ANY SHADY STUFF GO DOWN AT THE SCHVITZ?

Based on my less-than-pleasant experience with the Cleveland Mob Facebook group, I decided to go a different route to answer this question. I reached out to two east side guys who have lived, breathed and, most importantly, written about Cleveland's Mafia history: Rick Porrello and Frank Monastra.

Porrello is the author of five books on Northeast Ohio's Mafia ties. His best-known book is probably *To Kill the Irishman: The War that Crippled the Mafia*, which centers on notorious Irish gangster Danny Greene. In 2011, the book was turned into a motion picture called *Kill the Irishman*, which starred Ray Stevenson as Greene along with Christopher Walken and Val Kilmer.

Monastra has authored eight books, including *Portrait of John Scalish: The Mafia Boss No One Knew* and *Brancato: Mafia Street Boss.* Monastra is the grandson of Brancato.

I was excited to pick the brains of these two accomplished authors, hoping they would view me as a peer and not as some annoying Mafia fanboy. Rick and Frank got back to me within a few hours of emailing them, and sadly, neither one had come across any Schvitz mentions in their research.

In a way, the fact that neither guy had come across stories of Mafia men hanging in the Schvitz spoke to how special and secretive the Schvitz was. In my findings, there were many who alluded to nefarious activity that used to go down in the Schvitz—wild bachelor parties with prostitutes lined up and despicable acts out in the open or perhaps in one of the thirty dormitories that existed before the fire.

Some also swear that the Schvitz hadn't paid a water bill in years with an unspoken agreement with the Italian faction of the Cleveland Mafia who, according to some, controlled the water in the city for decades.

As you can imagine, nobody had specifics of what actually went down, but many claimed to have been there. Maybe time has faded the memories or maybe it was just guys wanting to impress their friends—the equivalent of half a million Clevelanders who proudly say they were at "Ten-Cent Beer Night" at old Cleveland Municipal Stadium in 1974.

So, was the Schvitz a Mafia hangout? Sure, that was one group that hung out there. It was also a hangout for judges, doctors, carpenters, factory workers, lawyers and fathers and sons. Most wiseguys were family guys too, so you wouldn't necessarily call church or temple a Mafia hangout.

And as it pertains to the Schvitz being a place where prostitution occurred, again, it happened from time to time at the occasional bachelor party, but it was more the exception than the rule. One anonymous Schvitzer claims an intimidating group of Russians tried to muscle in hookers as a regular part of the Schvitz shortly before Billy bought it in 2017, but that's mostly just hearsay.

Regardless, here are a few stories I came across that should whet the appetite of those looking to hear about some of the more colorful stories associated with the Schvitz.

Manny and Tommy Gambino

Gary Glazer, a Cleveland native and graduate of Cleveland Heights High, now residing in Philadelphia, has distinct memories of Manny and Tommy Gambino enjoying the Schvitz. The Gambinos were part of New York's "Five Families" of crime, including the Lucchese, Genovese, Bonanno and Colombo families.

"My father's cousin Irving Behrman was in the artificial flower business with Manny and Tommy Gambino in Manhattan," says Glazer.

> *They traveled west from their New York home base and often stopped in Cleveland on their sales trips. I was about twelve or fourteen at the time. On most of their visits, they would stay at our house in University Heights. I had a general idea of the Gambinos and that their uncle was Carlo Gambino. There were not a lot of detailed discussions about it. I remember*

Manny telling me he thought I looked like someone who worked for Robert Kennedy. I can't remember why I was dressed up, but I was in a three-piece suit, vest and all.

On several of their visits, they would go to the Schvitz. I was present at most, if not all, of their visits. On one occasion, I recall Manny kissing Irv on the lips when Irv arrived later than the rest of the group. I remember thinking that it looked slightly odd, but I made no comment about it.

Their visits lasted until about 1965. My family and I visited them in New York, and we went to the Copacabana in a scene reminiscent of the movie Goodfellas, *where Jerry Vale had dinner at a restaurant called Chez Vito. And then the visits just stopped cold. I heard nothing more from any of them until I heard on the news in 1974 that Manny had been kidnapped and murdered with his remains found sitting upright in a shallow grave near Newark Airport.*

My first thought was that this was the guy who stayed at our house, went to the Schvitz on several occasions with my father and me and even accompanied my parents and me when they dropped me off at Boy Scout camp in August 1964. We had been invited to his wedding, but my parents declined the invitation. At dinner once, my father asked Manny what he wanted to do with his life. He said his main goal was to have a trash route. My father said, "You went to Fordham University, and you want to be a garbage man?" Manny just chuckled.

Shondor Birns

Matt Bauman grew up in University Heights and has been schvitzing since the '70s. His grandfather Leo was also a Schvitz-goer, but more for business than pleasure.

"During the Great Depression, my grandfather, like a lot of Americans, couldn't find work, so he became a bookie, and his unofficial office became the Schvitz," says Bauman. "It was small bets, like penny bets, two-cent bets, the occasional nickel bets. He collected the money at the Schvitz and did the payouts there, too."

Eventually, an up-and-coming Shondor Birns got hold of what Lou was up to. Birns would later become a notorious crime figure in Cleveland, known for racketeering, theft and numbers. And the ambitious Birns wanted a piece of Leo's business.

"Shondor eventually found his way to the Schvitz and Grandpa Leo," says Bauman.

According to Bauman, Birns, along with some of his "goons," as Bauman describes them, asked Leo to take a ride with them. If you've seen enough gangster movies, taking a "ride" is never a good sign.

In the car, Birns tried to muscle (intimidate) his way into Leo's betting business, demanding a percentage of the profits. Leo, sensing the car ride could end in a beating or worse, kicked into fight-or-flight gear.

"As the car was making a left, Grandpa Leo opened one of the back passenger doors and jumped out of the car while it was still moving. He tucked and rolled and, besides a few scratches, came out relatively unscathed."

Bauman says Birns never bothered his grandpa Leo after that. Maybe it was the fact that Birns realized there were bigger fish to fry than a guy placing two-cent bets, or maybe Birns respected the chutzpah Leo showed when he voluntarily jumped out of a moving vehicle!

Birns was also known to hold a few meetings of his own in the back room at the Schvitz. "I remember Shondor being there," recalls Marc Seigel. "Yonkel would turn up the radio so nobody could hear what he and his guys were talking about."

Danny Greene

On Thursday, October 6, 1977, Gay Gold was straightening up around the Schvitz, folding towels and cleaning chairs and tables. A gentleman walked in, and Gay, being the friendly man he was, started making small talk. At around 3:15 p.m., the man looked at his watch and said to Gay, "Danny Greene just died."

Carmen Marconi, known for his role in tapping Danny Greene's phone, eventually learned of Greene's dentist appointment in Lyndhurst. Marconi's intel contributed to Greene's death in 1977. *Courtesy of Billy Buckholtz.*

Sure enough, Danny Greene had just been blown up in nearby Lyndhurst with a strategically placed car sitting next to his. Greene was walking out of a dentist appointment in a medical building when the car next to his exploded.

An anonymous source said that the man in the Schvitz that day had not planted the bomb himself but was part of the larger group who constructed the device.

RAIDED, SORT OF

According to the *Plain Dealer* story from March 6, 1969, the Schvitz was raided by three state liquor agents. Leading the group was area liquor enforcement chief Thomas J. Dominiak.

"Raided" may have been a stretch, as two of the three state liquor agents enjoyed steam baths and massages before sitting down for steaks, beer and whiskey. When in Rome! Dominiak joined the other two agents for dinner and afterward asked Jack "Yonkel" Gold if he had a liquor permit. Jack

Bathhouse Owner, Son Cited

Raiders Find Raw Side of Life

By HARRY STAINER

As about 75 men dressed in sheets and towels watched in disbelief, three customers at the Mount Pleasant Bath-House, 11409 Kinsman Road S.E., Tuesday night charged the bathhouse operator and his son with selling liquor illegally.

The three customers were state liquor agents led by Thomas J. Dominiak, area liquor enforcement chief.

Dominiak said two of the agents entered the bathhouse first, taking steam baths and massages before ordering steaks, beer and whisky. Dominiak joined the other two agents in the restaurant.

PLEADING INNOCENT yesterday were Jack Gold, 69, of 16818 Kenyon Road, Shaker Heights, the operator, who was charged with keeper and illegal sales, and his son, Gabriel (Gay) Gold, 47, of 3643 Linholm Road, Shaker Heights, charged with illegal sales. Municipal Court Judge Bernard J. Conway set April 4 for trial.

About 25 persons, most of them dressed in sheets and towels, were eating in the restaurant portion of the bathhouse at the time of the raid. Another 50 men were in steam baths or getting rubdowns. Most of them gathered to watch the arrests, agents said.

Dominiak said that when the agents finished eating, he asked Jack Gold if he had a liquor permit. He said Gold told him yes, apparently thinking it was a joke. He said he had trouble convincing Gold he was a state liquor agent.

AGENTS SELDOM go to such lengths to make a case. The last time they did was last April when 16 agents gathered for a dinner at the Executive Caterers, 27629 Chagrin Boulevard, Woodmere, to investigate complaints of liquor being sold at banquets.

Charged in that raid was Harlan J. Diamond, president of the catering company, and Leoncio C. Granda, its manager then. The case is still pending in Bedford Municipal Court and is expected to be heard next month.

Cosa Nostra Chief Jailed

PROVIDENCE, R.I. (AP) —Raymond L. S. Patriarca, identified in Senate testimony as New England chieftain of the Cosa Nostra, was taken into custody yesterday to begin serving a five-year sentence for conspiring to commit murder.

Patriarca was convicted on the conspiracy charge last year. The U.S. Supreme Court refused on Monday to review the case.

A 1969 article from the *Plain Dealer* where state liquor agents charged Jack "Yonkel" Gold and his son, Gabriel "Gay" Gold, with selling liquor illegally. Before arresting the Gold men, the liquor agents enjoyed a steam bath, massage, steak and whiskey. *Courtesy of the Plain Dealer.*

8

Two Soaked Nudes Toweled by Police

You can't very well eject someone by the coat collar when he has no coat on, two policemen learned early yesterday.

Or no pants either, for that matter.

Two men allegedly "causing a disturbance' in a bathhouse on the East Side were hauled away draped only in towels when their clothes could not be found.

All this began late Saturday night, according to police, with a round of taverns by the men.

They were identified as Joseph Ross, 44, of 1909 E. 123rd Street, and Nick Cirino, 43, of 827 London Road N. E.

Ross and Cirino wound up at the Mount Pleasant Russian Turkish Bath 11409 Kinsman Road S. E., where they disrobed.

Next events are uncertain, but at 1 a.m. police got a call from the bathhouse asking them to quiet a disturbance.

Patrolmen Anthony Modzelewski and Charles Fleischans were unable to get Ross and Cirino to quiet down, they said. And the men were unable to pick out their own clothes.

Finally, wearing towels, they were taken by patrol wagon to the Fourth District police station, 3600 E. 131st Street.

Friends brought them more suitable clothes there, and they were escorted the rest of the way to Central Station. They were released on bail, charged with intoxication and creating a disturbance.

This page: A 1960 article from the *Plain Dealer* that recounts how two men were arrested at the Schvitz for causing a disturbance. The men were escorted out by police wearing only towels, as they were too drunk to locate their clothes. They were eventually released on bail and charged with intoxication and creating a disturbance. *Courtesy of the* Plain Dealer.

replied with yes, thinking it was a joke. Dominiak said he had a tough time convincing Jack that he in fact was a state liquor agent. You can't blame Jack for his skepticism, as ball-busting and pranks are always part of the Schvitz experience.

Jack and his son Gay were charged with illegal sales, and a trial was set for April 4, 1969. It's unclear if the trial ever happened, as most likely Jack and Gold were probably ordered to pay a fine.

Chapter 10
SCHVITZIES

The Schvitz benefits from a small but mighty group of brand ambassadors who preach the gospel of steaks and sweat. Instead of handing out fliers on the street that say, "Come to the Schvitz!" these brand ambassadors, or Schvitz lobbyists, simply describe the experience to their friends, family and coworkers. If Taylor Swift has "Swifties," then the Schvitz has "Schvitzies." The following men are hardcore Schvitzies.

Josh Kramer

"I've perfected a sort of exercise I do with people when describing the Schvitz for the first time," says Josh Kramer, a Cleveland native now living in New York City. "Close your eyes and picture a stereotypically feminine spa experience. You probably think of a clean, welcoming atmosphere with soothing music in the background. There's a good chance women are relaxing, getting pedicures and maybe a couple of cucumbers are covering their eyes. There might be some wine, some small finger foods. All in all, a pretty chill vibe."

Kramer then asks the newbie to keep their eyes closed for the second part of the exercise.

> *Imagine there's a dial in front of you. The dial is set to "stereotypically feminine." Now, in your mind, turn that dial in the opposite direction. Actually, turn the dial so hard it breaks off.*

Substitute the relaxing and tranquil atmosphere with loud and boisterous. And replace the finger foods with heavy, artery-clogging foods like steaks and burgers. The Schvitz isn't so much relaxing as it is unique. Where else do you eat meals with nothing but a towel wrapped around your waist?

When I run people through my Schvitz exercise, usually they respond in one of three ways:

"I'm in. Steaks, beer, sweating? Let's go."

"Hmmm...sounds interesting, maybe I'll check it out sometime."

"This sounds awful. Why would you go to this?"

Josh has rented out the Schvitz for private parties for over ten years. In my research for this book, he was kind enough to send me the detailed spreadsheet he uses for his yearly Schvitz gathering. It's impressive, each spreadsheet color-coordinated with name, email, how the person paid, whether they got an add-on service like a massage or a platza, what potluck item they brought and, lastly, where people flew in from.

One thing is apparent: People travel for the Schvitz. It's a priority. For guys like Josh Kramer, his guests include people from New York, Florida, California and even Alaska. Who knew people would travel to Northeast Ohio to warm up?

Eric Golubitsky

"My father used to go to the bathhouses in Belarus because we didn't have a bathtub or shower at home. It was very ingrained in the culture."

Eric Golubitsky came to America with his siblings and parents in 1980. At the time, there was a lottery system that granted permission for one out of ten families to leave communist Russia. Golubitsky's family got lucky and were chosen, given a choice of three countries to immigrate to: Israel, Australia or America.

"My uncle worked at GE Lighting, which used to be out of Nela Park in East Cleveland. That was my parents' only reference to America, so they figured if my uncle lived and worked there, it probably wasn't half bad," Eric laughs as he recalls.

The Golubitsky family came to Cleveland and were part of a large contingent who settled in the east side suburbs like Mayfield Heights,

Eric Golubitsky's father and two sons. Golubitsky's father, who grew up in Belarus, was exposed to bathhouse culture at an early age. *Courtesy of Eric Golubitsky.*

Beachwood, Cleveland Heights and more. "Jewish Family Services Association of Cleveland placed families in many of the apartments in the Mayfield Heights area. Places like Gates Mills Towers and Marsol apartments."

Eventually, Golubitsky formed friendships with many of the other Russian Jewish boys in the apartment complexes. They were smart, hungry and eager to take advantage of everything America offered. The group eventually found their entrepreneurial itch with the mail-order computer boom of the mid-'90s.

Golubitsky remembers, "We all got into computers, building them and then doing mail orders to individuals and companies. It was very entrepreneurial. Going to computer expo shows and stores and pitching our products."

The expansion of the internet, along with the cost savings passed along to the consumer, was a recipe for success for Golubitsky and his friends. He dropped out of Miami University after one year, and soon he and his crew found the Schvitz, which for many, reminded them of home. "Every Thursday or Friday we would go after work, a group of Russian-Jewish entrepreneurs. It's so awesome. The herring in olive oil, cheese and kielbasa from places like Gallucci's or West Side Market. Every time you go it's a feast!"

Golubitsky has been going to the Schvitz for close to thirty years. Like fathers before him, he took his sons when they were old enough to appreciate the atmosphere and the locker room–like nature of the Schvitz. "I brought my boys when they were nine and eleven—old enough to appreciate it and mature enough to witness the debauchery."

Golubitsky has a photo of his dad and his boys sitting at a table in the dining room. It shows three generations of Schvitz men, starting in Belarus and ending up in Cleveland.

"A couple of times my dad brought his own platza branches," Golubitsky laughs as he recalls. "I'm pretty sure they told him to stop."

Ryan Kozak

Another Schvitz brand ambassador is Ryan Kozak, native Clevelander and senior managing director at Huntington Bank who has been organizing annual Schvitz holiday gatherings for coworkers for almost a decade. Kozak's first Schvitz experience was a memorable one. "The first time you go, you have no idea what you're doing. I was intimidated."

Kozak isn't alone in his first impression. Hospitality is thrown out the door when you enter the Schvitz. It's a figure-it-out-as-you-go type of thing. If you want hospitality, go to Pier W. Kozak continues: "So, we get there at like twelve or one, way too early in retrospect. We go up the stairs, find the locker room and change into our towels. Eventually, we find the staircase leading down to the steam room, but it's blocked by a stack of chairs. We moved the chairs, went downstairs and found the steam room."

Here's where that Schvitz hospitality, or lack thereof, enters. "We got in the steam room, and it wasn't on yet. A couple minutes later, a guy walked down and asked what we were doing. I said there was a stack of chairs blocking the stairway, so we moved them."

The guy turned out to be co-owner Greg Balogh. He responded to Kozak with "Well, if you see a stack of chairs blocking the staircase it probably means don't come down the fucking stairs!"

Kozak laughs when recalling the incident. "I figured out pretty quickly that Greg was his own kind of animal."

Paul Sobota

How do you know someone truly loves the Schvitz? Permanence is a good start.

Paul Sobota of Cleveland Heights started going to the Schvitz around 2008 with some friends who worked in the bars and restaurants around town. One night, they decided to keep the party going at a friend's apartment after they left the Schvitz. Feeling good from the combination of steam, steak and plenty of alcohol, an idea spawned that made perfect sense: Let's get Schvitz tattoos!

Sobota and his friends wasted no time. They called a friend who had been giving tattoos out of his apartment for a short while with the ask, and he obliged.

"We all went over there at about two in the morning. We gave him the concept, he made some stencils and got right to it," says Sobota. The tattoo on Sobota's left arm shows a T-bone steak in the shape of a heart with a sash going across it with the word "Schvitz" written out.

When Sobota awoke the next morning with a terrible headache and new art on his body, he said to himself, "I sure hope everyone else got the tattoo!" They did in fact, four guys altogether.

"Years later, I gave the same tattoo to my brother-in-law. It was one of my earliest tattoos and remains one of my favorites. It's pretty terrible technically, but what a great memory."

JOSH, ERIC, RYAN AND Paul are just a few of the hundreds, if not thousands, of Schvitzies who have descended on the building on Luke Avenue. There are a ton more Schvitz traditions out there. Whether it's an annual meetup, a tie to your family's native country or even an off-the-beaten-path holiday party, the Schvitz is an experience like no other. Its raving fans will tell you so.

Chapter 11

STAR TREATMENT

Like the stories of wild bachelor parties and Mafia meetups, the presence of local and even national celebrities who've swung by the Schvitz is mired in uncertainty. A few people told me Browns players would come the day after games to recover in the steam room and cold pool. Another person said Joe DiMaggio came by, at the invite of Doovy Kirschenbaum.

In recent years, the Schvitz has enjoyed visits from actor Oliver Cooper, best known for his roles in Showtime's *Californication* and Netflix's *Mindhunter*, along with comedian and *The Daily Show*'s Michael Kosta. Comedians coming to the Schvitz is nothing new.

Schvitz chef Paul Fierman and *The Daily Show*'s Michael Kosta. *Courtesy of Paul Fierman.*

"When Kip Addotta would be in town, he'd always come by the Schvitz," says Steve Presser. Addotta was a frequent guest on *The Tonight Show Starring Johnny Carson* and appeared on *The Mike Douglas Show* and the comedy gameshow *Make Me Laugh*.

Presser says, "It's funny, I remember when Addotta would be on local radio plugging whatever comedy club he was at that weekend, and he always mentioned he couldn't wait to go to the bathhouse. When the interviewer would ask him where it was, he'd say, 'I can't tell ya!'"

But perhaps the most talked-about Schvitz visits come from a combination of an Oscar-winning actor, two comedians who stumbled upon it and a local Cleveland television legend.

Actor Matthew McConaughey

In 2017, *White Boy Rick* began filming in Cleveland. The film was based loosely on Richard Wershe Jr., who became the youngest informant ever at fourteen. In a weird, backhanded compliment, Cleveland was chosen (in addition to the tax breaks) because it resembled 1980s Detroit.

Filming took place at more than twenty-five locations around Ohio, and Matthew McConaughey, who played Richard Wershe Sr., eventually found his way to the Schvitz.

"I'm not sure how he found out about us, but I think he came alone the first time," says Paul Rotman, of Pepper Pike. "After that, he came maybe four or five more times with people from the movie. He rented it out once or twice."

For the most part, other Schvitz-goers left McConaughey alone. But some couldn't help but say, "Hey, you look like Matthew McConaughey!" According to Rotman, McConaughey responded on more than one occasion with, "You know I've been told that a few times…and it's gotten me laid on more than one occasion."

Comedians T.J. Miller and Cash Levy

When comedians are in Northeast Ohio to perform stand-up, it's usually at one of two clubs: Hilarities 4th Street Theatre or the Cleveland Improv, which now goes under the name the Funny Bone on the west bank of the flats.

These comedians have a lot of time to kill. Some will get up early and do radio interviews to promote the shows that weekend, but other than that, they're pretty much free until 6:00 or 7:00 p.m. Most of them go to the usual spots: They'll walk down to the Rock & Roll Hall of Fame, grab an Uber to the West Side Market or catch a Guardians afternoon game if there's a homestand.

In November 2019, comedians T.J. Miller and Cash Levy were in town to perform at Hilarities 4th Street Theatre. Both were like Bob Seger crooning, "strung out from the road" and needed a little place to unwind.

After a bit of Googling "Cleveland sauna and steam rooms" only to find many were expensive spa-type places or ones associated with pricey hotels, they found the Schvitz. T.J. gave the Schvitz a call and had a brief conversation with Billy.

Ring, ring…

Billy: This is the Schvitz.

T.J.: Yeah, are you guys open?

Billy: What?! Whaddya you think? We're on the phone.

T.J., still unsure how the Schvitz operated, asked Billy about the operation. Billy described the features: a steam room, cold plunge, food and men only (at least for this particular night). Billy then asked T.J. where he was from, and when T.J. responded with New York, the two started talking about the Russian and Turkish Baths on 10th Street. Once T.J. deciphered it wasn't a gay club, he and Cash decided to give it a try.

Miller and Levy took an Uber to the Schvitz and were quite puzzled during the commute. Boarded-up and foreclosed homes provided the not-so-scenic backdrop this cold November night. When they arrived, they still weren't sure this was a good idea.

"We told the Uber driver to hang out for a second because based on the outside and the neighborhood we were in, we didn't know if we'd be staying," said Levy. "When we made it to the top of the stairs, the first thing we saw was fifty men in towels, eating steak, smoking. T.J. and I had never seen anything like it."

Levy knew there was something inherently special and old-school about the building he had entered.

"It's just madness. Cigars, alcohol, huge steaks. These were guys who were not body-conscious in the least. They were the real deal. Even though I didn't know anyone in there except T.J., I thought to myself, 'I would go to war with these guys.'"

Levy sensed the camaraderie of the men in the dining room, and as the night progressed, he began to realize he'd stumbled onto something pretty special. "There's an old soul to the place; you can feel it, and it can't be duplicated. You can't make another Fenway Park or Wrigley Field. Stadiums and comedy clubs do this all the time. They move a block over and try to sell it as the same thing, but it feels different. The new Yankee Stadium is nice, but it's not Yankee Stadium."

Lil' John Rinaldi

Where in the world is...Lil' John Rinaldi? Bonus points if you sang it Rockapella style.

Lil' John Rinaldi is a Cleveland icon. I won't go into the history of Big Chuck and Lil' John, because that is its own book. All you need to know is the four-foot-three-inch spark plug was a longtime Schvitzer who grew up just around the corner.

"I grew up on East 110th and Woodland," says Rinaldi. "I remember passing by it on the bus to and from school." Rinaldi graduated from John Adams High School, about three minutes from the Schvitz. Like many Cleveland sons, he knew of the building on Luke Avenue from his dad.

"My dad used to go all the time, but ironically, I never went with him. I didn't go until I think 1967 or 1968, after I graduated from Ohio State. I went with my brother and some friends." Rinaldi remembers an intimidating presence greeting him in the parking lot.

"When I pulled in, this big Black guy with guns on both hips told me he'd park my car," says Rinaldi. "I went to John Adams, so it's not like I wasn't around Black people, but this guy meant business. When he told me he'd park my car, I thought to myself, 'Well, I guess he's parking my car,'" Rinaldi remembers. "Before the fire, the staircase to get up was just three little steps, so I walked in and I remember peering into the locker room, and it was dark. The guy at the front asked if I wanted a lock for my locker, and I said sure. I was given a little lock and a key. I found out the same key opened all the locks!" Rinaldi laughs.

Lil' John Rinaldi in 2024. The famous Cleveland television personality grew up just a few minutes from the Schvitz, attending John Adams High School. *Courtesy of John Skrtic.*

"Tuesdays, at least back then, were Jew and Italian nights. I remember steak was the only entree you could order; they hadn't introduced salmon or other types of fish yet. You could get the steak large, medium or small, with or without garlic."

Like many Schvitzers, Rinaldi remembers wearing the stench of garlic as a badge of honor that told everyone, through their

To answer the question of Where in the world is...Lil' John Rinaldi? The answer is Florida. He spends ten to eleven months out of the year there, only returning to Cleveland for the winter holidays. I pounded the pavement to reach Rinaldi. He was my white whale! A big thanks to all the people who assisted in the search.

nostrils, that you had recently been to the Schvitz. "The garlic stayed on you for days. You reeked of it."

Rinaldi indulged in the simple pleasures of the experience—the platzas, the food, the fellowship and, of course, the massages. "They had these Russian masseurs who pummeled you," says Rinaldi. "I always got deep tissue massages, and these guys did not disappoint!"

The only feature Rinaldi didn't indulge in was the cold pool. "Out of the twenty or so guys I went with, maybe three jumped in; just wasn't our thing. There are two reasons I never got in the cold pool. One, the water was black. Two, I can't swim!"

Not being able to swim and being four feet, three inches is a bad combination! As a short guy myself at five feet, five inches, I think I can make that assumption. And of course, I asked if Big Chuck ever tagged along. Rinaldi said no. Damn. Going to the Schvitz with Big Chuck and Lil' John would've been *peak* Cleveland.

▪ ▪ ▪ ▪ ▪ ▪ ▪

This story has no relation to the Schvitz, but this is a book mostly Clevelanders will read, so please indulge me.

My wife and I got married in January 2020 in her hometown of Knoxville, Tennessee. The morning after our wedding, my cousin Terry texted my wife and said, "I just saw Lil' John eating at our hotel's continental breakfast!" Maybe it was the whirlwind of the wedding the day before, but my wife and I thought he meant Lil Jon the rapper. You know, "Turn Down for What" and "Get Low" Lil Jon.

I Googled "Lil Jon tour 2020," and it didn't look like he was touring, let alone in Knoxville. I also thought it was weird that he, as an accomplished entertainer, was staying at a Best Western in Knoxville (my cousin Terry always opts for the great rates). Suddenly it hit me. Terry meant Lil' John Rinaldi! When I told my wife, she replied, "Wait, so Cleveland has a Lil Jon, too?!" I told her not *A* Lil' John, *THEE* Lil' John. Show some respect.

Chapter 12
LADIES' DAY

When we reintroduced Ladies' Day, someone said I should be tarred, feathered and dragged down Kinsman.
—Billy Buckholtz

This comment was made on, you guessed it, Facebook, when the Schvitz announced it was doing Ladies' Days again. Who knows, maybe it was the same guy from the Cleveland Mob Facebook group who told me to leave the Schvitz alone and go the hell away.

Ladies' Day is as much a part of the Schvitz history as anything else. When the Schvitz opened in 1927, the original ad in *The Jewish Independent* boasted "Wednesday's for Ladies."

In the Mark and Greg Balogh era of the Schvitz (1996–2016), Ladies' Day fell by the wayside, with only a handful taking place, mostly for very close friends and family. The Schvitz under the Balogh brothers was raw, unpolished and hypermasculine to an extent. Many had gotten associated with the experience being men only. Today, more women than ever are going to the Schvitz and getting the physical and social benefits men have enjoyed for decades.

I've Got the Greatest Job in the World

"My wife, Debbie, went on a Ladies' Day with Jo Kirschenbaum and decided she wanted to get a massage. Through a few friends, she heard the masseur was a blind gentleman named Charlie," says Steve Presser.

"Not only did Debbie feel bad the man was blind but that he was posted up in the dark confines of the Schvitz's makeshift massage room with cots lined up next to the lockers. But since he was blind anyway, maybe she was overthinking it," Presser chuckles as he recalls.

What happens next is a Schvitz story for the ages.

Since Debbie knew there would be no lingering eyes fixated on her, she casually walked toward the massage table naked, with only her sheet under her arm. She got a massage and generously tipped Charlie, mostly because she felt bad for his lot in life.

A few minutes later, Debbie saw Charlie in the dining room stacking Cokes in the refrigerator. Debbie thought it was weird he so effortlessly completed the task, but she also knew blind people know certain routines and have a feel for objects, so she didn't question it. A few minutes later, she saw Charlie writing something down. That's when she knew something was up.

"It turns out, Charlie called in sick that day!" Presser laughs. "The fill-in guy wasn't blind at all. Not only did he get to massage a beautiful naked woman, but he was tipped generously for doing so. That guy went home saying to himself, 'I've got the greatest job in the world.'"

Debbie can't help but smile when she recalls the story.

> *I remember when I walked up to him, butt-naked have you, and he sort of turned away. Then before I got on the massage table, I dropped the sheet on the ground, and he proceeded to pick it up and cover me with it. I thought, "What does it matter if I'm not covered up?" I didn't think too much of it and just settled in for the massage.*
>
> *Like Steve said, after I saw him putting Cokes in the fridge and writing stuff down, I knew something was up. We were paying up at the end when one of the Schvitz workers casually said, "Charlie? He was sick today."*

Debbie recalls another time when nakedness and the Schvitz went hand in hand.

"I went on a Ladies' Day with Jo, and we were all in the steam room. I can't remember how many girls, but a decent group," Debbie recalls. "At the time, Billy was the platza guy, and he was just kind of hanging in the corner of the steam room. I think both he and our group weren't quite sure how to proceed. Would a female be coming in to relieve him, or was he the guy that day?"

Both sides were apprehensive to make a move, but one brave soul, confident in her body, decided to break the ice. "A younger girl stood up, who had a great body and was wearing nothing but a thong bikini, and said, 'I'd like a platza.' She went first, and then we all followed her lead!"

For Billy, it was just another day at the job. He had been giving platzas since he was a child, though mostly to old Jewish men.

"Billy was great," says Debbie. "Totally professional and laughed that he was simply a worker on the assembly line. Afterward, he remarked, 'Either I'm in heaven…or I'm going to hell.'"

I Love My Husband, but I Wouldn't Want to Take Him Here

Lauren Calevich is an event planner in Cleveland. In 2024, she was part of a team that helped plan Cleveland Kurentovanje, a Slovenian Mardi Gras–type festival that celebrates chasing winter away in anticipation of spring. Though in February it's still very much winter, especially temperature-wise, in Northeast Ohio, you have to appreciate the Slovenian optimism.

After the event, Calevich and a few coworkers were discussing how Cleveland has so many under-the-radar cultural traditions. Though thousands of Slovenians show up annually for Kurentovanje, many still don't know about it. Someone chimed in, "Yeah, Kurentovanje is such a hidden gem, kinda like the Schvitz."

A couple of the girls in Calevich's group had been there, but most had not. As the conversation progressed, everyone agreed that not only was the Schvitz a Cleveland curiosity, but it was a bucket-list item they'd always wanted to check out.

"I grew up in the inner city, in the Superior–St. Clair area near East 55th," says Calevich. "I don't get too freaked out by 'bad' neighborhoods, but I do have to say when you first see the Schvitz from the outside it's a little puzzling."

Everyone, and I mean *everyone*, including men, no matter how tough they think they are, has a similar first impression when they come upon the building:

Is this it?
No way this is it.
Is this place abandoned?
Are you sure this building isn't condemned?

"But when you get inside, it's awesome," says Calevich.

For Calevich, the Schvitz represented an equal playing field where even the most body-conscious person could feel at ease. "What I loved right off the bat was there was no pressure. Everyone was just comfortable with who they were. There were itty-bitty girls and plus-sized girls of all ages, and I felt like it was a safe space. It was very freeing."

Calevich and her group were all in. Many enjoyed the platzas, the massages, the steam, the cold pool and, of course, the patio.

The view pulling into the Schvitz. Most first-timers think, "No way this can be it" or "Is this safe?" *Courtesy of Jason Morris.*

"It was a beautiful day and unseasonably warm for April. We were out on the patio with our tops off, and it was no big deal." Calevich adds that even though she went with a group, there was no pressure to do everything together.

"You kind of make your own adventure at the Schvitz," says Calevich. "If you wanna steam you can go steam, or if you wanna get a massage you can do that too. Or if you want to hang on the patio that's cool, too."

Calevich, nearing forty, represents a demographic you don't often associate with the Schvitz. But just as fathers took their sons or grandfathers took their grandsons, the notion of mothers taking their daughters or grandmothers taking their granddaughters is just as plausible.

With more and more Ladies' Days on the calendar, a new generation will find the building on Luke Avenue that's been around for nearly one hundred years. Inevitably, some of the millennials and Gen Z women who choose to start families will eventually take their daughters to the Schvitz.

A few loyal Schvitz men I've interviewed don't like the idea that the Schvitz is now more inclusive than ever. This includes the gentleman who wanted to tar and feather Billy. For some old-school guys, the Schvitz is a guys' thing, one of the last places where "men can be men," a place where you can eat, drink, smoke and let it all hang out away sans girlfriends and wives. Ironically, some of the female Schvitz enthusiasts feel the same way.

"I love my husband, but I wouldn't want to take him here," comments Calevich. "It was just so freeing being around women of all shapes, sizes and ages." Calevich is right. There aren't too many patios in Cleveland where you can hang out topless.

Cash Levy, the comedian we met in the previous chapter, has respect and admiration for the women who come to the Schvitz. "If you're a girl and you come to *this*, you're pretty fuckin' cool."

Chapter 13

PUBLIC ENEMY NO. 1

If the Schvitz were the FBI, Doug Trattner would be No. 1 on their most wanted list. At least in 2011.

Trattner penned "Sweat the Small Stuff: Craving Steak and Nakedness? Time to Find the Schvitz" for *Cleveland SCENE*. The almost 1,200-word essay is an entertaining and accurate account of experiencing the Schvitz from a reliable source. Not only is Trattner an accomplished writer, but he's also Jewish and from the east side.

"I probably first went when I was eleven years old and always thought the place was interesting. It was almost like an unofficial bar mitzvah." Trattner added, "You have to remember, 2011ish was the peak hipster chef scene around Cleveland. Guys like Michael Symon, Jonathan Sawyer and Rocco Whalen all loved it."

Trattner thought it was so interesting that he decided to give Clevelanders a sneak peek into one of Cleveland's most mysterious places. Up to that point, not much had been written about the Schvitz, at least not in a publication with as much readership as *SCENE*.

"Even before the story came out, I could tell it was going to strike a nerve with people," says Trattner. Variations of "Really? I don't know if that's a good idea" and "What are you doing? Not sure if they want that" were popping up. And when the article did come out, the response was, well, passionate.

"*SCENE* was an early adopter of digital articles having a comments section, so you can imagine some of the stuff on there. Things got nasty and personal, quickly. A few threats here and there, but I didn't take any of them seriously. The comments section back then is what Twitter is like today."

SCENE has always been a liberal publication that values free speech. Initially, the comment section was left up. But as the feedback got more colorful, the publication decided to disable the comment section. In a way, Trattner's story broke the internet, way before breaking the internet became a thing. One comment that is still up on *SCENE*'s website reads, "The schvitz has not changed since 1927 and this is what makes it so great. As for the author, I think he should have written about Chuckie Cheese, not our beloved Schvitz." The post was made by the reader "Need a large towel," so do with that what you will.

At the time, Trattner had been writing professionally for about a decade, switching over to the literary world from practicing law. The article became one of his most popular, if not most popular, stories to date.

"As a writer, it's always a nice confidence boost to have people talking about your story. I didn't get the whole 'boys club secrecy' behind the Schvitz. I thought it was a little selfish. Why shouldn't people know about this place?"

SCENE magazine in 2011. The cover story, written by Doug Trattner, outraged then-owner Mark Balogh, who preferred the Schvitz stay under the radar. When Balogh learned of the story, he proceeded to throw a chair across the dining room. *Courtesy of* SCENE.

When the story came out, Mark Balogh, who co-owned the Schvitz at the time with his brother Greg, had a less-than-positive response to the free and unwanted publicity. "Mark was furious. He threw one of the dining room chairs across the room," says Billy. "He was adamant that Doug would never be allowed in again, cursing him up and down."

Billy, who was about six years away from buying the Schvitz from Mark, couldn't understand the anger. He knew Mark wanted to keep the place low-key, but this was free advertising and a whole new set of eyeballs who never knew this place was even in Cleveland.

After Mark's chair-throwing tirade, Billy calmly pulled him aside and tried to talk him off the ledge. "I told Mark, this is pure gold. I understand you're pissed off, but why not laugh and be pissed off all the way to the bank?"

The vitriol from Balogh was interesting, considering six years earlier the *Plain Dealer* had run a story on the Schvitz that ran on the front page. From the tone of the *PD*'s article, it seemed that Mark had agreed to it, which said, "Mark Balogh said word of mouth is all he needs. He's got the biggest, driest, hottest box in town."

Was retaliation ever waged against Trattner from Mark? Not that Trattner remembers.

"I don't believe they ever reached out to me, though I did hear the *SCENE* cover (which depicts a drawing of a man's gut with a towel wrapped around it holding a lit cigar) was taped up somewhere with some sort of 'don't let this guy in' message."

Looking back, 2011 wasn't that long ago. The Schvitz under Mark and Greg Balogh was a sweaty speakeasy. No website, no social media, no frills. Just the people who knew about it. And if you wanted to check it out, you had to come with someone who was in good standing. The *SCENE* magazine article brought unwanted attention in the short term but piqued curiosity for the long term. Doug Trattner hasn't been back to the Schvitz since.

Chapter 14

DESTINATION WEDDING

By now it's been established that the Schvitz is a sacred place, so it only makes sense that two people decide to pledge their forever love in the company of friends, family, steaks and steam.

The Schvitz doesn't have members; it has characters. And Bill Seymour is no exception. Seymour, originally from Kirtland, Ohio, is a workaholic. From 2000 to 2018, he not only worked a full-time job as an HR professional, but he also worked weekends cutting trees with his company, Seymour Tree Service.

"I'd do my normal 9–5, and then in the evenings I would drive around and do estimates on jobs and scope out projects," Seymour says. "Then on the weekends, I'd work Saturday and Sunday doing tree removal."

I asked him why he went through this kind of grind, considering his corporate job probably paid the bills and was demanding enough.

"I grew up poor, on welfare, and never wanted my kids to go through that. I told my first wife—you raise the kids, and I'll provide for all of us. It's just how I'm built."

With his grueling seven-day work schedule, one luxury he did give himself was visiting the Schvitz.

"An old friend of mine named Maury invited me back in 1999. We went after work, and I, like most first-timers, was in utter shock pulling into what looked like an abandoned building," Seymour fondly recalls.

It didn't take long for Seymour to get hooked. Since that fateful day over twenty-five years ago, he's gone roughly fifteen times a year since. When you

The Schvitz

East 116th Street & Luke Avenue Cleveland, Ohio

- ***A windowless brick building on the westside of East 116th street directly across Luke Avenue, and just past 3286 East 116th Street. PLEASE LOOK ON-LINE FIRST, to get your directions straight or call Bill Seymour! LeRoy is the guard in the fenced in parking lot to greet you!***

Nelva and Bill are extremely excited about living the second half of our lives as one family who are blessed with four fabulous children we cherish greatly! We want to take this next step in a unique fashion no one else may claim on their life's resume.

We will exchange wedding vows at the Cleveland Schvitz, which is a historical pastime!

SCHVITZ

The "Bathhouse or Cleveland Schvitz" was founded in 1927 and is a Yiddish term meaning sweat. Since the doors initially opened in the 20's the Schvitz was considered a private club for primarily Jewish and Italian males to associate over social and business dealings. Sometimes close confidants and family members would attend these gatherings. As the years past the Schvitz would sometimes host activities for women and only recently began hosting an annual Co-Ed Valentine's Day party.

Countless influential people and celebrities have visited the Schvitz over the decades including the famed actor Matthew McConaughey, who made several visits while working on a film in Cleveland, Ohio.

To this day generations of family & friends routinely meet during the winter months at this private club known as the Cleveland Schvitz to take a steam, share stories, break bread, drink spirits, smoke cigars, and enjoy the finest steaks in town at this historical bathhouse.

Nelva and Bill love this atmosphere and would truly appreciate our beloved "cool" family and friends to enjoy a bit of history as we cement ours!

ATTIRE

There is no need for you to dress up for this event! Please wear comfortable clothes and bring a bathing suit and flip flops if you intend on enjoying the steam room---despite what stories you may have heard no one will be naked during your visit.

If you are not interested in taking a steam, which the steam room is ***HIGHLY*** recommended, you should still change into shorts or something comfortable to make the most of your visit.

FOOD

The Schvitz is known for its steaks, but you will also have other choices of food including burgers and seafood. Your dinner and basic set up is covered already!

Please bring with you whatever wine or alcohol you like to drink---most domestic beers are available for purchase at the Schvitz.

We guarantee you will love your inaugural visit to the Cleveland Schvitz!

The PDF wedding invite sent out by Billy Seymour and Nelva Smith. The invite states, "We want to take this next step in a unique fashion no one else may claim on their life's resume." *Courtesy of Billy Seymour.*

do the math, it adds up to someone who doesn't just like the Schvitz but loves it with all his heart.

When Seymour decided to remarry in 2020, the second marriage for both him and his fiancée, Nelva Smith, there was only one place to do it. "Billy [Buckholtz] had done Ladies' Days and coed days for a few years, so I pitched the idea to him. He loved it." But did his soon-to-be-wife share in the excitement?

"Nelva is a great partner and knew how much the Schvitz meant to me, and she had become a fan herself as we went to a few of the coed days together. She was all in. The steam, the massages, the platza—a real trooper. I'm not just saying this because she shares my Schvitz appreciation, but every day being married to her has been like a holiday."

With that, a select group of—in Billy's words—"cool" family and friends were emailed a wedding PDF invite for Super Bowl Sunday, February 20, 2020. Billy laid it all out as to what to expect, from pulling into the building, attire, food options and so on.

Seymour, dressed in a bow tie, white Under Armour shirt and swimming trunks, said "I do" to Nelva, dressed in a cover-up with a swimsuit underneath. Their wedding officiant, an attorney Nelva worked with, was dressed impeccably in a Hawaiian T-shirt and shorts.

"It was the second marriage for both Billy and I, so I wasn't interested in doing a big wedding with a white dress and all that stuff," says Smith. "I would've been fine just going to the courthouse, but when Billy mentioned the Schvitz and offered to plan the whole thing, I was all in!"

The day was memorable for all parties as Billy and Nelva tied the knot in the upstairs dining room. Sneaking it in just before COVID shut down the world five weeks later, Billy and Nelva enjoyed steaks, steam and the accompaniment of friends and family, many of them first-timers. And on this particular occasion, the Schvitz was given a woman's touch.

"Billy's wife, Michele, went out of her way to make the day nice," says Nelva. "She put some nice flowers on the tables and made specialty drinks, which I appreciated."

Billy Seymour and Nelva Smith's wedding party enjoying the steam room. For many, it was their first time. This coed experience is more common now, as the Schvitz offers coed days. *Courtesy of Billy Seymour.*

Billy Seymour and Nelva Smith were married at the Schvitz on February 2, 2020, just six weeks before the COVID pandemic. It was the second marriage for both, and Seymour commented, "If it's good enough for Matthew McConaughey, it's good enough for us!" *Courtesy of Billy Seymour.*

Nelva doesn't know this, but she's a hero to men in Northeast Ohio who try to get their wives to indulge in the Schvitz's simple pleasures. Some women scoff at the idea of going to the Schvitz, let alone getting married there. But maybe her husband sums it up best: "If it's good enough for Matthew McConaughey, it's good enough for us!"

Chapter 15

THE SCHVITZ'S FUTURE: A SWOT ANALYSIS

What will the Schvitz look like five, ten, fifty years from now? To summarize some of the themes we've talked about, I thought a short SWOT (Strengths, Weaknesses, Opportunities, Threats) analysis could help us understand what the Schvitz can capitalize on and what it needs to watch out for.

Strengths

Tradition and Loyalty

Passionate devotion is on the Schvitz's side. The Schvitzies, no matter if they're in Cleveland or have moved away, will make it a point to get to the Schvitz, even if it's only once a year. The men who've been coming, whether for fifty years or five years, are fiercely loyal. Even as Northeast Ohio baby boomers enter their twilight years and begin to pass away, the sons, grandsons and nephews of these men will carry on the tradition.

Brand Equity

Another strength the Schvitz has going for itself is its one-of-a-kind experience. You can't franchise a place with so much history, or

"McDonalds-ize," it as one Schvitzer said. If a similar experience opened in an affluent suburb like Pepper Pike or Rocky River, people may go, but it couldn't be called the Schvitz. The brand equity the Schvitz has developed for nearly one hundred years allows it to charge a premium price for an experience that can be imitated but never duplicated.

Doug Trattner, who still writes for *Cleveland SCENE*, shared a text thread on Twitter about Nighttown in Cleveland Heights, which recently closed its doors for good. The same sentiment is true with the Schvitz: "A restaurant is not four walls and a menu: it's people, it's history, it's routine and habit."

The curiosity associated with the Schvitz is still one of its biggest assets. In my interviewing people for this book, countless people responded with, "Oh, I've heard about it and have always wanted to go" or "Is that the place where you get naked and eat steak?"

Along the way, a few steam rooms in Cleveland have come and gone, the most popular being Elsner's Steak & Steam, which operated from the early '60s to 2006 and was located in Shaker Heights. The first ad for Elsner's appeared in the *Cleveland Jewish Independent* newspaper in 1960, boasting "The Most Complete and Modern Facilities for Your Health." Another ad in the *Plain Dealer* in 1961 touted Elsner's as "A Complete Physical Therapy Operation" and "not just another 'Turkish Bath.'"

The arrival of Elsner's was also indicative of where Clevelanders were heading and how areas had changed.

"In 1959, five eastern suburbs led the charge to rename Kinsman to Chagrin. When you reached the Cleveland and Shaker Heights border, the street name changed from Kinsman to Chagrin," says Karl Brunjes, city planner for the Cleveland Landmarks Commission.

Brunjes goes on to describe how the area had mostly transitioned from a Hungarian to an African American neighborhood. Specifically, members of the Kinsman Jewish Center and St. Margaret of Hungary Catholic Church were moving to the more eastern suburbs as more African Americans came to Cleveland as part of the Second Great Migration between 1940 and 1970.

The street name change from Kinsman to Chagrin could be attributed to encouraging development along a main road, while at the same time, it could be said that racial undertones and hints of redlining were at play.

Despite what you think of the Kinsman to Chagrin name change, Elsner's provided an interesting dichotomy to what the Schvitz provided. Some men were Schvitz purists, never stepping foot in Elsner's. Others enjoyed both places, never feeling a particular loyalty to one over the other.

OVERWORKED?
TAKE A TWO HOUR VACATION—SUNSHINE AND ALL
ONLY $5.50
• PINE STEAM ROOM • HOT ROOM
• QUARTZ SUN LAMP • OIL MASSAGE
• WHIRLPOOL • GYMNAZION
COME OUT FEELING EXHILARATED AND WONDERFUL
ELSNER'S Health Center
20116 Chagrin Blvd. Cleveland 22
At the end of the Van Aken Rapid SK 2-0330
Open Daily from 10 A. M. Closed Mondays

ELSNER'S HEALTH CENTER
FOR MEN ONLY
20116 Chagrin Blvd. Shaker Hts. 22, Ohio
SK 2-0330 SK 2-0331
The Most Complete And Modern Facilities For Your Health.
TIRED? IRRITABLE? Do you feel the need to just relax and let the tensions fall away? A hot pine-steam bath, a luxurious massage by trained experienced personnel, a sun bath, or, perhaps a whirlpool bath, full body, will allow you to forget your problems and tensions. Try us!
Tues. and Thurs. .... 10 A.M. to 10 P.M.
Wed. Fri. and Sat. .... 10 A.M. to 8 P.M.
Sunday .... 9 A.M. to 4 P.M.
Closed Monday
Ample private parking in the rear off Lomond Blvd.
Not a club and not a plan. Come as frequently or infrequently as you desire.

Top: An ad for Elsner's Health Center from 1961. *Courtesy of the* Plain Dealer.

Bottom: An ad for Elsner's Health Center from sometime in the 1960s. *Courtesy of the Samuel H. Miller Digital Archive of the* Cleveland Jewish News.

Elsner's had more space to work with than the Schvitz, having three dining rooms that each held forty to fifty people. They also had a pine steam room, sauna, whirlpool and small gymnasium (spelled *gymnaziom* in the *Plain Dealer* ad). Like the Schvitz, Elsner's offered massages as part of their services but no platzas or cold pool.

One person Elsner's left an impression on was Dylan Fallon, who graduated from Shaker Heights High in 2003. Fallon co-founded Ninja City, a kitchen and bar with multiple locations around Northeast Ohio that blends Asian cuisine and American pub grub. Fallon worked at Elsner's and Matsu, a Japanese restaurant that resided in Shaker Square, in his teen years. "I remember Elsner's always got good crowds for Sunday brunches," Fallon recalls. "The eggs benedict was always a favorite, and you couldn't beat the Oreo ice cream cake."

Keith Arian remembers Elsner's well, more for the food than the sweat. "I went once or twice to the steam and sauna room there, and I think one time I went because the Schvitz was temporarily closed because of a water or electrical issue."

Like Fallon, Arian remembers the meals more than anything: "When I first got married in the early '80s, my wife and I had a 'membership,' which

Dylan Fallon, who co-founded Ninja City in 2014, worked at Elsner's Steak and Steam in his teen years. Fallon cites Elsner's as a place where he got an informal education in food and culture. *Courtesy of* Shaker Life Magazine.

meant we had a small locker to keep our liquor in when we went there for dinner. We would eat there about once a month with family or friends. Like the Schvitz, Elsner's were known for their steaks, and the salad was accompanied by a bacon, egg and onion served in a three-compartment spinning thing-a-ma-jig."

Like the Schvitz, Elsner's was where some of Cleveland's most interesting people descended upon. "I learned so much there," says Dylan Fallon. "I didn't have a lot of aunts and uncles, so the customers at Elsner's became my family and teachers. The vibe was an adult locker room of hearty, well-educated people. Doctors, lawyers, blue-collar professions. I am Korean and adopted, so Elsner's was a place where I learned about inclusivity and how to act with manners and confidence."

Emerging Health Trends

With sauna use and cold plunging making a significant dent in mainstream culture, the Schvitz is in a unique position to offer, for most, a one-time hot and cold experience you can't find anywhere else in Northeast Ohio.

A few modern places have popped up in recent years, including North Coast Cryo in Beachwood, which offers cryotherapy and an infrared sauna. The same goes for Cryoactive Wellness in Rocky River. These places provide up-to-date, modern, clean environments for sweating and freezing but don't offer the camaraderie, tradition or Fred Flintstone steaks the Schvitz is known for.

In addition to emerging health trends, it's also very en vogue to hang in saunas and steam rooms. In fact, some of the nation's top power players are asking the same questions men from Northeast Ohio have asked their buddies for decades: "Hey, can you get me in?"

The Diplomatic Sauna Society, established around 2008, is one of the most sought-after invites in D.C.'s famed Beltway. Located in the basement of the Finnish Embassy, the DSS provides the opportunity for delegates, journalists, civil servants and academics to network in a healthier setting rather than a stuffy hotel bar or fancy restaurant. The group sweats once a month with roughly fifteen to twenty invite-only members, with each gender having their own sauna so they can choose to go nude if they like.

Those who brave the heat of the sauna in the Finnish Embassy are rewarded with a diploma. The diploma reads, "Membership in the Society is awarded only to individuals who have demonstrated extraordinary sisu (grit) by conversing effortlessly and eloquently in the 180-degree Fahrenheit heat of the embassy's diplomatic sauna."

It makes sense that the Finnish Embassy would have a sauna, as in Finland there are roughly 3.3 million saunas for a population of 5.5 million people.

Weaknesses

Price

The price tag of a Schvitz visit could be a weakness or a strength, depending on who you ask and, more importantly, how you value disposable income. As of 2024, it's $150 for the steam and the meal. This doesn't include tipping the parking lot attendant or staff or ancillary features like getting a platza or massage.

With the Schvitz's brand equity, they can charge this amount based on the value for which the customers believe it holds. Though the price might be too high for some, some appreciate the now-streamlined approach.

"When Greg and Mark ran the Schvitz, you never knew how much you were going to pay at the end of the night," Alan Mancuso smiles as he recalls. "The guy in front of you would say, 'I had a steak and three beers,' and Mark would say, 'All right, seventy bucks.' Then the guy behind him would say the same thing, and Mark would reply, 'Ninety bucks.'"

The debate over the value you're getting at the Schvitz depends on what you consider a good deal and what ambiance you want with your steak. In 2024, Marble Room Steaks and Raw Bar was named the most expensive restaurant in Ohio by FoodLove.com. An average night for two will run you anywhere between $200 and $500.

In comparison, the Detroit Schvitz enacts an à la carte system where it's forty dollars for admission, which gets you a locker, towels and access to the saunas and pool. Ancillary optional purchases include robes for rent (five dollars), along with sandals and locks for purchase (ten dollars each). If you decide you're hungry and want to eat, you can add meals like soup, salads, hamburgers and, of course, steaks. Depending on the cut, the steaks run around thirty-five dollars.

A Schvitzer who preferred to remain anonymous said he understands the challenge from both the Schvitz's point of view and the customer. "I understand that $150 is a lot of money for some people, and I also understand the Schvitz is trying to run a business. I think it's worth it because you can stay there all day if you like. You can steam, hang in the pool, on the patio, eat, drink. There's a lot to do."

Changing Tastes

The Schvitz indulgence is similar to another bedrock of Jewish culture: Jewish delis. Bathhouses like the Schvitz and Jewish delis are now more the exception than the rule. In 1931, there were thousands of Jewish delis in the five boroughs of New York. Today, there are around 150 in all of North America.

"If you think about it, both the Schvitz and Jewish delis are gluttonous experiences," says Josh Kramer. "With the Schvitz, it's ripping into the biggest steak you've ever seen, and with the Jewish deli, it's the overstuffed corned beef sandwiches or pastrami on rye."

In the 2014 documentary *Deli Man*, which chronicles the charms and challenges of Jewish-inspired delicatessens, Michael Wex, author of *Born to Kvetch* and thought leader of Yiddish culture, describes the men who used to hang out in the delis and the steam rooms: "Who hung out in delicatessens is the same bums who hung out in the schvitz, the steam bath, which is bookies, and Jewish criminals, and Jewish-aspiring criminals who pretended to be synagogue presidents."

"The Schvitz, like Jewish delis, is a relic of an immigrant past that no longer exists," says David Sax, who was also featured in *Deli Man* and penned the 2010 book *Save the Deli: In Search of Perfect Pastrami, Crusty Rye, and the Heart of Jewish Delicatessen*. "What makes an old-school Schvitz so great is walking into a place frozen in time."

Dietary-wise, many Americans have gone the vegetarian route. Though the Schvitz offers fish and vegetarian options, some can't get the image of the massive steaks out of their minds, which may keep some away.

Opportunities

Women

The biggest opportunity the Schvitz has for lasting growth and profitability is the somewhat recent re-addition of Ladies' Days and the even more recent Coed Days. As previously mentioned, Ladies' Days were few and far between under the ownership of Gay Gold and Mark Balogh. Now, two or three times a month, a group of women or a group of men and women can experience the steak and steam.

Even more important than the Schvitzies might be the ladies, especially those in the Gen Z and Millennial demographics. These women represent a newer customer base who may one day bring their daughters and granddaughters, the same way old Jewish and Russian men brought their sons and grandsons. Paddy Lynch of the Detroit Schvitz has said women have become the backbone of the business—even more so than the old-timers.

"The women have built their own Schvitz traditions, and they prioritize self-care," says Lynch. "We do a women-only brunch on Sundays from twelve to four, and some days we have to turn people away."

Today, the Cleveland Schvitz is slowly gaining a reputation as a fun girls' day or night out. It's also an off-the-beaten-path place to hold a bachelorette party. It might not be Las Vegas or Nashville, but it can be just as memorable and less expensive.

Top: An ad for the Schvitz's Valentine's Coed Day in 2024. Some Schvitz purists scoff at the idea of mixing genders in the steam room. But for others, it's the equivalent of a fun pool party. *Courtesy of Cleveland Schvitz's Facebook page.*

Bottom: A recent ad for the Schvitz in 2025. Ladies' Days and Coed Days are now much more common than in previous years. *Courtesy of Cleveland Schvitz's Facebook page.*

Urban Revitalization

"Can you imagine walking to the Schvitz?" Josh Kramer, the Schvitzie with the impressive spreadsheets, asked me this hypothetical question. Now that I think about it, not one person I interviewed said they walked to the Schvitz and then walked home. It doesn't look like Mount Pleasant will experience an Ohio City or Tremont gentrification transformation anytime soon, but it does raise the question of whether gentrification around the Schvitz would be good or bad for business.

At first glance, it would seem that more people who can safely get to the Schvitz on foot would be a good thing. But in another sense, part of the Schvitz's revenue is derived from its parking fee, where customers tip the attendant anywhere from five to fifty dollars.

The common benefits of gentrification, like increased property values and business growth, could spur a rebirth for the mostly neglected area surrounding the Schvitz. However, some long-standing residents of the Kinsman area prefer the area just how it is and stand the chance of being priced out if rent and property taxes increase.

Threats

Since the Schvitz has been around for nearly one hundred years, it's safe to say it has weathered the storm of almost every possible threat. Like most businesses in 2020, the Schvitz had to adapt to the COVID-19 pandemic, and it did, putting in a new ventilation system and an outdoor patio area. They masked up, got creative and moved forward. Changing times are nothing new to the building on Luke Avenue.

"In the '80s, MTV was a game changer," said Billy. "People stayed home to get their music fix and weren't coming out as much to the clubs and bars to see live acts. At the same time, health clubs and country clubs started installing saunas and steam rooms."

We've covered some possible threats already in the "weaknesses" section (pricing, changing tastes), but here are a few that could impact the Schvitz in the next ten to twenty years.

Age and Dilapidation

The bathhouses built in Cleveland during the late 1800s and early 1900s have stood the test of time, and besides the fire that took place in 1992, the Schvitz has held up nicely. Sure, from the outside the building looks utilitarian more so than inviting, but inside the bones of the Schvitz remain strong.

As far as dilapidation, as long as the Schvitz isn't neglected, it should continue. Billy's somewhat recent renovations of new bathrooms upstairs and the patio outside are examples of the care put into keeping the Schvitz in good shape for years to come.

One might ask why the Schvitz, given its age and historical significance, hasn't been deemed an Ohio historical landmark. Though it might be possible for the Schvitz to qualify for a tax break through the Ohio Historic Preservation Tax Credit (OHPTC) program, it's believed the Schvitz just wants to be left alone, without interference from the city or state. Chances are if the Schvitz did become a historical landmark, it would have to satisfy the requirements of certain inspections to qualify for the tax credit. The Schvitz doesn't need those headaches.

In-Home Saunas

The uptick in people opting for their own home saunas can be attributed to a few things, mostly convenience and COVID. When the world shut down, people realized how much they loved and relied on a good sweat.

According to *Estonian Saunas Magazine*, sales of the popular HUUM sauna skyrocketed by 221 percent in March 2020. Another popular European sauna brand, Iglucraft, whose claim to fame is selling a home sauna to David Beckham, reported that in the same month, it had already sold 60 percent of the total saunas it sold in all of 2019.

Now, these numbers reflect what was going on in Europe during the pandemic, but America didn't seem to be far off. The explosion of in-home saunas and sauna culture in general has remained steady; the ads I get when I scroll through Instagram stories tell me as much.

Some could say the in-home sauna trend could be compared to the trend of watching movies on streaming apps at home rather than going to a theater. Since COVID, a lot of us have gotten a lot more homey, as more people work remotely. We can now work, sweat and watch the latest movies without leaving our homes. This isn't just a Schvitz threat; it's an overall leisure and entertainment threat.

The debate could go on and on about how the Schvitz will survive and what to look out for. The aspects mentioned here were just a couple of things to think about. Maybe they'd make good conversation over steak and sweat!

CONCLUSION

When Kevin "Noodles" Lynch left the Schvitz as a masseur in 2007, he knew he'd be back, but on the other side of the massage table as a guest. The life lessons and relationships he made there would last a lifetime.

"In 2008, I threw a big Schvitz party with about forty people," recalls Lynch. "It was a mix of friends, family and many of the people I had massaged." The Schvitz meant a lot to Lynch, and he wanted to express his gratitude with a toast.

Lynch, feeling good from the steam, company and a few too many glasses of whiskey, gave an impromptu toast in front of his Schvitz brethren. Now, it wasn't uncommon for Schvitz men to give long-winded, out-of-the-blue toasts in the dining room, but Lynch's toast was centered on everyone being a "diamond in the rough."

"I don't know what got into me—probably the scotch—but I started to refer to everyone I was with as a diamond in the rough. Mark and Greg owned it at the time, so I said they were diamonds in the rough, and my dad was there; he was a diamond in the rough, too," laughs Lynch. As Lynch's speech rambled on to the room full of toweled guests, he finally wound things down by expressing how much the Schvitz meant to him and how much it had taught him. As he was struggling to find the right words, someone in the dining room yelled, "We get it, Noodles. This place is a diamond in the rough. Now sit down!"

One of the reasons people feel such affinity for the building on Luke Avenue is because the Schvitz is a lot like us—flawed and imperfect. The outside of the Schvitz is nothing to gush over; it looks a little road-weary, like dark circles under our eyes. The parking lot isn't made of smoothed-over asphalt; it's gravel with no distinct spots and too many potholes to count. Our potholes show up in the form of insecurities, regrets and flaws within our own character. Maybe it was a bad relationship or career choice. The Schvitz isn't polished, and neither are the men and women who enter. But it stirs something inside of us. The steam awakens our senses and permeates our souls. Author Jason Glaser, who I've referred to a few times, is spot-on with his thoughts after experiencing the first real deep sweat of his life: "I felt lighter, clearer, more alive. It was as if a veil had been lifted, and I was seeing the world in high definition for the first time."

It Was Like Coming Home to a Home I'd Never Been to Before

Zoe Apisdorf walked into the Schvitz for the first time on May 19, 2024. It was Coed Day, and Apisdorf and some of her coworkers at Rustbelt Riders, a local composting company in Cleveland, decided to make a day of it.

When Apisdorf walked up the stairs, she was greeted at the front counter by Billy. He asked her what she wanted to eat and what her name was. She replied with steak and then said her name. Billy, now seventy-two, keeps a mental Rolodex of the names and faces that have passed through the Schvitz.

"Apisdorf?…Apisdorf…was your dad Harry?" asked Billy. Zoe smiled and said, "Yes, that was him. He loved this place." As Billy and Zoe talked a little more, she began to tear up. Billy remembered her dad. Now she was at the Schvitz, to help remember him too.

Harry Apisdorf died in 2009 at age fifty. Zoe, his only child with his wife, Leslie, was nineteen when he passed. She remembers her dad as a fun, playful and kind man who was even more fun and playful when he came home from his monthly visit at the Schvitz.

"My parents used to call me 'Inspector Gadget' because of my curious nature," recalls Apisdorf. "The Schvitz was always something I knew my dad went to, but that I couldn't go, like an adult thing. My dad was always silly and playful, but I feel like he was always in an even better mood when he came home from this magical place I knew nothing about."

Harry and Leslie Apisdorf had their own business in used equipment financing. Leslie hung back and took care of a lot of the paperwork behind the scenes, while Harry was out in front shaking hands and making deals. Zoe remembers her dad, an affable mensch who seemed to always leave people better off than when he found them, as a man who always gave people a little extra for whatever they needed.

"My dad had the innate ability to sense what someone was lacking," says Zoe. "Whether it was cash, kindness or just a space to get away, he had this empathetic way to him. There were a lot of times he'd invite a colleague or acquaintance out to our property in Russell Township [located in nearby Geauga County] to spend the day with us."

Zoe and her father shared mischievous personalities and loved pulling pranks on each other. Harry, being the adult, was often one step ahead. But Zoe got one over on him that most Schvitzers would appreciate.

"My dad and I would do these little campouts in the living room where we'd bring a mattress out and I would sleep there, and he would usually doze off before me," says Zoe. "We had a fireplace in the living room, and it was something I always looked forward to. One night, when my dad fell asleep, I painted his toenails white. I thought it was the funniest thing! White toenail polish was in then, so it was probably the late '90s or early 2000s."

The father-daughter campout happened on a Friday, and the next day, unaware that his pristine porcelain toenails were now colored a creamy white, Harry went to the Schvitz. Something was off. In the steam room, people looked at him curiously, like he was "funny"—funny being gay or queer. Finally, he looked down at his feet. He couldn't help but smile. The student had become the master!

After Zoe had reminisced with Billy about her dad, she joined her fellow Rustbelt Riders in enjoying everything the Schvitz had to offer and made sure to load up on electrolytes before hitting the steam.

"I asked for a whole bowl of pickles, no questions or no funny looks," said Zoe. "It was done with great service and care. It fucking rocked."

Zoe couldn't help but feel a sense of connection to her dad as she navigated through the locker room, dining room and down to the steam room and cold plunge pool. She asked herself in the dining room if this was the table her dad would have picked. In the steam room, she made her way up to the benches and thought, "Is this where he would've steamed?" These were the same rooms he walked about decades earlier, and now in a small way, she was right there with him.

From left to right: Kevin "Noodles" Lynch, David Porris and Paul Rotman celebrating Paul's birthday at the Schvitz. Porris, who's been coming to the Schvitz religiously every Friday since the mid-1970s, will often ask newcomers in the steam room, "What have you got to do that's better than this?" *Courtesy of Kevin Lynch.*

"We store a lot of grief in our bodies from past trauma," says Zoe. "I know I do when it comes to my dad. There's a gap that can never be filled. I'm sad he won't be there if I decide to one day get married or have kids, but the Schvitz helps with the healing process. The heat, the cold, the atmosphere. Even Billy just remembering him means a lot to me."

I was fortunate enough to be at the Schvitz and meet Zoe on this special day. As we were on the patio, taking in an unseasonably nice Cleveland day, she quipped, "It was like coming home to a home I'd never been to before."

In the same vein, the Schvitz has acted as a second home to a steam room legend. Since 1974 or 1975, he can't quite remember, David Porris of Beachwood has been coming to the Schvitz every Friday. Five decades of sweating have served him well. At seventy-four, he's got long gray hair tied back in a ponytail and a lean figure to go with it. The Schvitz has kept him healthy, both in the physical and social sense. The Schvitz is just what he does on Fridays, much the same way other guys have Tuesday night bowling leagues or Saturday night poker games.

David counts only a handful of times he's missed his Friday Schvitz appointment—a few family weddings, but that's about it. "One time the Rockettes came to Cleveland. My wife went; I opted for the Schvitz," Porris laughs.

David is known for a saying at the Schvitz. It's actually on one of the podcast episodes that comedians T.J. Miller and Cash Levy recorded back in 2019. If there's a newcomer to the Schvitz and they get to talking with Porris in the steam room, he'll ask them a rhetorical question as they sit and sweat together: "What have you got to do that's better than this?"

EPILOGUE

I was nineteen when I finally got the chance to visit the Schvitz. I owe that experience to Jo Kirschenbaum and Mark Balogh. The occasion was a private, one-time-only Ladies' Day that paid tribute to macher David "Doovy" Kirschenbaum, a family friend and longtime Schvitzer who helped get the Schvitz back up and running from the fire in 1992.

Part of the longtime rationale for keeping women out was that the neighborhood was not "safe" for women to drive to. My first drive down this side of Martin Luther King Drive to 116th, past Buckeye, was in the late spring of 2008. I had never been in this neighborhood before, ever. Sandwiched in the intersection of Woodland Hills, Buckeye and Mount Pleasant, these were neighborhoods that no one of my generation would recognize.

My mother and I drove together. I was dismayed by the number of surrounding abandoned houses and boarded-up storefronts. I learned the Schvitz, this place my dad has casually gone to thousands of times, was a few blocks away from the infamous serial killer rapist Anthony Sowell's house. How could the "childhood real-life boys-only club" of my dreams be surrounded by poverty, pain and suffering? That's a story for another book.

We pulled up to a closed chain-link gate guarding the shittiest-looking building, half covered with ivy and overgrown weeds. "This is it?" I mumbled to my mom, disgusted. A super friendly man who I would come to know and love, Leroy or Mr. Lee, welcomed us. He had an army of kittens meowing at his feet. "My babies," he said affectionately. He wished us well and went

A view from the top of the steam room. Many fill the metal buckets (lined up on the second to last bench) with cold water and pour it over their heads so as not to overheat. *Courtesy of the author.*

back to his kittens. He spoke into a two-way radio with Mark and Greg Balogh, two brothers I only knew of as the Schvitz dudes.

I had such mixed emotions. I was anxious but underwhelmed, desperately trying to reset my expectations, trying to prepare myself for utter heartbreak. Something told me the fantasy might not be as good as reality. My childhood self may have blown the "top-secret Schvitz" out of proportion.

Walking up to the top of the stairs felt and smelled familiar—cigarettes and deli. Somewhere between Grandpa's basement and Broadway Bagels. Naked centerfolds cluttered the walls, complemented by fumes of stale cigarettes and cigar smoke.

I somehow managed to get my suit and towel on and walked back down the stairs to the shower room—a place I had seen only in pictures. I noticed the famous cold plunge pool first, and the child-like mystique returned, vanishing my dissatisfaction from the drive there. I dipped one chilly toe in the cold plunge and thought, "Cool, but where is the sauna?"

My eyes caught a wooden door. That must be it. By now everyone but my mom and I were upstairs eating, and soon a few lady Schvitzer regulars

The higher you sit, the hotter it gets. Many first-timers have learned that when you sit at the top bench, leaning back against the scalding hot brick wall is not a good idea. *Courtesy of the author.*

joined us. My mom and I were pairing bits of what we thought we were "supposed to do." It weirdly occurred to me that no ladies know what to "do" here. I remembered something about throwing water on the rocks to create steam, so I did it. My mom thought she could re-create my dad's platza, so we did it, or at least attempted to. We had a Schvitzin' good time. When I finally got too hot, I emphatically plunged into the coldest water I can remember being brave enough to enter. As I ran out quickly, I felt a little unsteady but euphoric. I'd repeat this process several times. It was intuitive. It was joyous. I was hooked. I remember thinking, "I cannot wait to do this again," which quickly shattered knowing I might never get to.

Spoiler alert: I did. Some years later, the Schvitz would leave Mark Balogh's hands (rest in peace, Mark) and the keys would be given to my dad. A natural passing of the torch, ushering in a new era.

My dad started getting a lot of phone calls from women who wanted a women's-only private party. We did not know how much this interest would expand over those first few years. They instituted a coed Valentine's Day experience for couples that continues to be well attended. They also made

Staying in the tradition of fathers and grandfathers bringing their sons and grandsons to the Schvitz. Present owner Billy Buckholtz and his grandson Arthur. *Courtesy of Sam Buckholtz.*

some large construction changes to accommodate more parties in the dining room. I am so proud of my dad. He has helped usher the Schvitz into the modern era while holding on to what makes it sacred. He has also welcomed many women into the experience so we can find our own joy and sacredness.

There are not many places that have stuck around for nearly one hundred years. I love the history of the Schvitz and hope my son will enjoy it the same way thousands of others have. The Schvitz is part of me, the same way it's part of all the people you've read about. And I have to ask, if you haven't sweated in the Schvitz, have you really sweated? If the answer is no, it's time for you to start making your own stories. Towel optional.

—Samantha Buckholtz
CNM
Cleveland Heights, Ohio

ACKNOWLEDGEMENTS

Stay on the path. Fall off the path. Get back on the path.
It's as simple and as hard as that.
—*Brad Stulberg*

My first book was a love letter to copywriting, my second book was a love letter to stand-up and this is a love letter to steam.

Writing a book changes you as a person. I'm guessing parents go through this with newborns. You don't know what you're getting into until you're in it. When I started writing this book in early 2024, there were some challenges. Thanks to the family and friends who helped me stay on the path.

To Lauren, what else can I say; Dori and I would be lost without you. Thank you for putting up with our stubborn and needy ways.

To Mom, for all the love and support. Many people, especially Cameron, feel your encouragement on Facebook.

To Dad, for your passion for cold plunges. Let's activate those cold shock proteins.

To Jay, in the process of not wanting to be great, you stumbled upon it. Continue to fail your way to success.

To Mikester, for all the support and joining the dog dad club. Stella is lucky to have you.

To Tina and Grandma, for somehow putting up with over thirty years of Womack humor. You are angels among mortals.

To Denise and David, the best in-laws a guy could ask for. I admire your humility and how you achieved it.

To Jason, Sarah, Anna, Kelvin and Murphy, for all the love sent from Nashville and New Orleans. And the Murphy pictures and videos, let's be honest.

To the Mayfield McDonald's crew, Adam, Frank and Mums. I hope Tony's there.

To the Herb's dad crew, Steve, Evan and Cameron. Good-looking group and even better guys.

To Zach, for being the connector in making this happen. They'll blow it in the playoffs.

To Luca and Dave, the 705 boys. Yeahhh!

To Terry, Jen and Ryan, for always showing up.

To Billy, for opening the doors to the Schvitz not just to me, but for more people than ever.

To Sam, thanks for being so passionate about the project. Your enthusiasm helped me on many days.

To Mikey and Michele, for all the behind-the-scenes support that often goes unnoticed.

To "Noodles," for sharing your stories and being a cheerleader for the project.

To Josh, for your impeccable spreadsheets and insights. Maybe you should write the sequel!

To John and Mark and the Cleveland Public Library, great resources and even better people.

To Brant, Darcy and Wendy, for sharing wonderful memories of your dad and grandfather.

And a special thanks to the following people for their time and insight: Paul Rotman, Sarah Rotman, M.P., Ben Balogh, Greg Balogh, Ryan Supler, Andrew Zuccaro, Doug Guth, Ryan McKinley, Mark Cousineau, Paul Hadley, Eric Mack, Blake Johns, Richard Johns, Leah Santosuosso, Gary Glazer, Seth Briskin, Alan Altshuld, Eric Novello, Beth Piwkowksi, Doug Trattner, Bill Seymour, Nelva Smith, Tony "Doc" Sumodi, Matt Bauman, Keith Arian, Danny Kirschenbaum, Jo Kirschenbaum Cowan, Lynn Gross, Caryn Gross, Amy Moniot, Charlie Mintz, Elise Free, Steve Presser, Debbie Presser, Sam Allard, Eric Sandy, Eric Golubitsky, Zoe Apisdorf, Paul-Jason Silver, Lil' John Rinaldi, Lauren Calevich, Steph Rienzi, Sam Musser, Bryon MacWilliams, Al Mancuso, David Porris, Paul Fierman, Malik Moore, Deborah Gray, Paddy Lynch, Tony Vento, Rocco Whalen, Lauren McGrath, Nate Pangrace, Michael DeAloia, Michael Wex, Cash Levy, David Sax, Dylan Fallon, Jim Sollisch, Brett Becker, Kyle Wells, Sean Martin, Daniel Rosenblum, Miriam Rosenblum, Marc Seigel and Jeremy Conway.

BIBLIOGRAPHY

Articles

BC & LJ Show. bigchuckliljohn.com/history--bios.html.

Beautiful on Raw. "Beauty Tool for Glowing Complexion." www.beautifulonraw.com/Skin_Exfoliator_Tool.html.

Buckeye Beat. "Wild Horses." https://www.buckeyebeat.com/wildhorses.html.

Case Western Reserve University Encyclopedia of Cleveland History. "Bath Houses." case.edu/ech/articles/b/bath-houses.

———. "East Ohio Gas Co. Explosion and Fire." case.edu/ech/articles/e/east-ohio-gas-co-explosion-and-fire.

———. "Mount Pleasant." case.edu/ech/articles/m/mount-pleasant.

Cleveland.com. "Roy H. Curtis." August 1, 2014. obits.cleveland.com/us/obituaries/cleveland/name/roy-curtis-obituary?id=10894794.

Cleveland Historical. "Broadway Bath House, 1940." clevelandhistorical.org/index.php/files/show/1559.

———. "Clark Avenue Bath House, ca. 1930s." clevelandhistorical.org/index.php/files/show/1563.

———. "Coit Road Bath House, 1929." clevelandhistorical.org/index.php/files/show/1560.

Cleveland Jewish News. "David Kirschenbaum." June 22, 2006. www.clevelandjewishnews.com/archives/david-kirschenbaum/article_6ac7aa66-36e8-5287-bd40-73227fb17070.html.

———. "Eugene Phinick." January 20, 2016. www.clevelandjewishnews.com/community/lifecycles/obituaries/eugene-phinick/article_decd1bf4-0e47-11e2-8ccf-0019bb2963f4.html.

———. "Kraus, William J. 'Bill.'" January 21, 2004. www.clevelandjewishnews.com/archives/kraus-william-j-bill/article_9aa56b16-4852-5b0c-83e9-8b0f979eb6ae.html.

———. "Mark Talisman, Who Helped Write Jackson-Vanik Amendment to Free Soviet Jews, Dead at 78." July 17, 2019. www.clevelandjewishnews.com/news/local_news/mark-talisman-who-helped-write-jackson-vanik-amendment-to-free-soviet-jews-dead-at-78/article_e23e5750-a646-11e9-bdbb-4325228f783e.html.

———. "Schvitz Has Exclusion Policy." October 4, 2011. www.clevelandjewishnews.com/archives/schvitz-has-exclusion-policy/article_2a32e2c8-adaf-5d20-a28c-ed062a083019.html.

Farkas, Karen. "Indians Fans Bring Goats to Progressive Field in Hopes of Continuing Chicago Cubs Curse." Cleveland.com, October 24, 2016. www.cleveland.com/metro/2016/10/indians_fan_brings_goats_to_pr.htm.

Feldmar, Jamie. "Chef Jonathon Sawyer's Favorite Restaurants in Cleveland, Ohio." Tastingtable.com, April 15, 2015. www.tastingtable.com/690411/chef-jonathon-sawyer-favorite-restaurants-cleveland.

Gaspaire, Brent. "Redlining (1937–)." Blackpast.org, December 28, 2012. www.blackpast.org/african-american-history/redlining-1937.

Greenberg, Gail. "Morison Avenue Bath House." Clevelandjewishhistory.net, April 30, 2020. www.clevelandjewishhistory.net/places/bathhouse.html.

Hanson, Debbie. "Tony Sumodi: Mischievous Youth Becomes Iconoclast Engineer." Cleveland Seniors, May 2010. www.clevelandseniors.com/people/tony-sumodi.htm.

History. "Chicago Cubs Win First World Series Title Since 1908, Snapping 'Curse.'" November 3, 2021. www.history.com/search?q=Curse+of+the+billy+goat.

Krueger, Alyson. "'Whatever Happens in the Sauna Stays in the Sauna': Diplomacy, Conducted in the Nude: The Finnish Embassy Offers One of the Hottest Invitations in Washington: A Chance to Discuss Serious Topics in a Sauna." *New York Times*, August 25, 2024. www.nytimes.com/2024/08/25/style/sauna-finnish-embassy-washington.html.

Levick, Jeffrey. "Sweatin' with the Oldies." Clevelandjewishnews.com, January 31, 2002. www.clevelandjewishnews.com/archives/sweatin-with-the-oldies/article_c2d7809c-97d6-5828-841a-7eebac3fb6e3.html.

Mentz, Zach. "Cleveland Restaurant Named Most Expensive in Ohio, Report Says." Cleveland.com, March 29, 2024. www.cleveland.com/

news/2024/03/cleveland-restaurant-named-most-expensive-in-ohio-report-says.html#:~:text=Located%20at%20623%20Euclid%20Avenue%20in%20Cleveland%2C%20Marble%20Room's%20menu,according%20to%20Marble%20Room's%20menu.

Merwin, Ted. "How a Religious Revival Fed the Demise of the Midtown Kosher Deli." *New York Jewish Week*, September 7, 2023. www.jta.org/2023/09/07/ideas/how-a-religious-revival-fed-the-demise-of-the-midtown-kosher-deli.

Miller, T.J. "Holy Schvitz." *Cashing in with T.J. Miller* (podcast), December 10, 2019. podcasts.apple.com/us/podcast/holy-schvitz/id512774441?i=1000459171761.

Olympia Daily. "The History of the Bath House as a Cultural Gathering Space." www.olympiadaily.com/journal/the-history-of-the-bath-house-as-a-cultural-gathering-space.

Rang, Adam. "After Global Lockdowns Began, Sauna Stove Sales Surged a Staggering 221%." Medium, May 11, 2020. medium.com/estoniansaunas.

Richter, G.M. "Greek Strigil." In *Greek, Etruscan and Roman Bronzes* (Lindemann Press, 2008). healthandfitnesshistory.com/ancient-fitness-tools/greek-strigil.

Rolnick, Josh. "Sweating in the Cleveland Schvitz." Forward.com, March 7, 2012. forward.com/news/152601/sweating-in-the-cleveland-schvitz.

Rotman, Michael, and Chris Roy. "Lincoln Park Baths." Cleveland Historical, 2009. clevelandhistorical.org/items/show/154.

Russian and Turkish Baths. www.russianandturkishbaths.com.

Sansone, D. "Greek Strigil." In *Greek Athletics and the Genesis of Sport* (University of California Press, 1992). healthandfitnesshistory.com/ancient-fitness-tools/greek-strigil.

Seidman, Irv. "Going to the Schvitz." *Cleveland Jewish News*, June 10, 2015. www.clevelandjewishhistory.net/events/seidman-schvitz.htm.

St. Mary, Rob. "Detroit Bath House the Schvitz Gets a New Life: New Skin for the Old Steam Room." *Detroit Metro Times*, November 1, 2017. www.metrotimes.com/arts/detroit-bath-house-the-schvitz-gets-a-new-life-6750324.

Trattner, Doug. "Sweat the Small Stuff." Clevescene.com, February 23, 2011. www.clevescene.com/food-drink/sweat-the-small-stuff-2355330.

Williams, Michael. "The Schvitz." Acontinuouslean.com, December 29, 2008. www.acontinuouslean.com/2008/12/29/the-schvitz.

Books

Boteach, Rabbi Shumley. *The Broken American Male: And How to Fix Him*. St. Martin's Press, 2008.

Glaser, Justin. *Sweat: Uncovering Your Body's Hidden Superpower*. Self-published, 2023.

MacWilliams, Bryon. *With Light Steam: A Personal Journey Through the Russian Baths*. Northern Illinois University Press, 2014.

Pantzar, Katja. *The Finnish Way: Finding Courage, Wellness, and Happiness Through the Power of Sisu*. Tarcherperigee, 2018.

Rubinstein, Judah, and Jane Avner. *Merging Traditions: Jewish Life in Cleveland*. Kent State University Press, 2004.

Ryan, W.F. *The Bathhouse at Midnight: An Historical Survey of Magic and Divination in Russia*. Penn State University Press, 1999.

Sweeney, Jim. *What's the Deal with Dead Man's Curve?: And Other Really Good Questions About Cleveland*. Gray & Company, Publishers, 2023.

Film, TV and YouTube

Deli Man. Directed by Erik Greenberg Anjou, performances by Steve Auerbach, Adam Caslow and Alan Dershowitz. Cohen Media Group, 2014.

The Shvitz. Directed by Jonathan Berman. Five Points Media, 1993.

ABOUT THE AUTHOR

Joshua Womack is a senior copywriter who lives in Downtown Cleveland, Ohio, with his wife, Lauren, and their dog Dori. This is his third book.